Praise for
One Month to Live

"Through the ups and downs, routines and regimens of our daily existence, we can become complacent, even bored, with life. But God never meant for life to be boring. And in *One Month to Live,* Kerry and Chris Shook remind us of the true depth and meaning that God has in store for each of our lives. No matter where you are in your walk with God, this book will reveal to you a fresh and much-needed perspective. And at the end of this thirty-day journey, you will discover exactly what it means to truly live—daily…creatively…passionately!"

> —ED YOUNG, Senior and Founding Pastor of Fellowship Church and author of *Outrageous, Contagious Joy*

"Too many people live with regrets, missed opportunities, and dormant dreams. You don't have to be one of them. Your life will be different if you apply the transformational principles in Kerry and Chris Shook's *One Month to Live.*"

> —CRAIG GROESCHEL, Founding Pastor of Lifechurch.tv and author of *Confessions of a Pastor*

"*One Month to Live* by Kerry and Chris Shook will add value to the life of every person who reads it. The questions asked and the 'Make It Count Moments' in this book will stir your soul and inspire you to begin, today, to make the rest of your life more meaningful. What Kerry and Chris present in *One Month to Live* could be life altering."

> —KEN BLANCHARD, author of *The One Minute Manager* and *Know Can Do!*

"If you want new urgency, fresh purpose, and a sharper focus for your life, then this book is for you. Read it and your future may be changed forever!"

> —LEE STROBEL, author of *The Case for the Real Jesus*

"Regardless of where you are on your spiritual journey, *One Month to Live* will challenge you to passionately live the life you were made for and leave an eternal legacy."

> —BILL HYBELS, best-selling author and Senior Pastor of Willow Creek Community Church

About the Authors

KERRY AND CHRIS SHOOK founded Fellowship of The Woodlands in 1993 with eight people. Since then, the church has grown to more than fifteen thousand people, becoming one of the largest and most influential churches in America. Its main campus is in The Woodlands, outside of Houston, Texas.

Striving to eliminate the barriers that keep people from experiencing a relationship with Jesus Christ, Kerry and Chris believe that church should be engaging and life changing. They have touched thousands of under-resourced people locally and in countries around the world through the missions and ministries of Fellowship of The Woodlands.

Their weekly television program is broadcast to millions of viewers. It can be seen in all fifty states and more than two hundred countries worldwide.

Kerry and Chris have been married for nearly twenty-five years and have four children.

ONE MONTH TO live

ONE
MONTH
TO *live*

THIRTY DAYS
TO A
NO-REGRETS LIFE

KERRY & CHRIS SHOOK

WATERBROOK
PRESS

ONE MONTH TO LIVE
PUBLISHED BY WATERBROOK PRESS
12265 Oracle Boulevard, Suite 200
Colorado Springs, Colorado 80921

Trade Paperback ISBN 978-0-307-73096-1
eBook ISBN 978-0-307-44495-0

Published in the United States by WaterBrook Multnomah, an imprint of the Crown Publishing Group, a division of Penguin Random House LLC, New York.

The Library of Congress has cataloged the hardcover edition as follows:
Shook, Kerry.
    One month to live : thirty days to a no-regrets life / Kerry and Chris Shook. — 1st ed.
        p. cm.
    1. Christian life. I. Shook, Chris. II. Title.
    BV4501.3.S564 2008
    248.4—dc22

                                    2007042529

Printed in the United States of America
2016

10 9

For Ryan, Josh, Megan, and Steven

As we have raised you, in many ways you have raised us.
We pray that you will always live with no regrets.

Contents

Principle 1

Live Passionately

Principle 2

Love Completely

Principle 3
Learn Humbly

Principle 4
Leave Boldly

Foreword

Nothing focuses a person's priorities in life like learning he is about to die. Many of us would suddenly realize we have spent our lives on things that were not very important. So many of us waste our lives with "when and then" thinking, believing that "when" this or that happens, "then" we will really start living and do something for God that really matters.

That approach is guaranteed to leave you with regrets. At the end of your life, the only thing that will matter is whether you accomplished God's purpose for your life. Jesus was just twelve when He said, "I must be about My Father's business." Just twenty-one years later, He could say to the Father, "I have completed the work You gave me to do." If we all had that kind of focus and concentration in our lives, there's no telling what God would accomplish in the world!

The fear of death paralyzes most people, preventing them from taking the risks necessary to fulfill God's plan for their lives. Kerry and Chris Shook want you to grasp an amazing insight: embracing your mortality sets you free to live a meaningful and satisfying life without regret. As He did with Queen Esther, God put each of us in the world "for such a time as this." *One Month to Live* is a great way to discover the purposeful, joyful, abundant life God created you to enjoy!

Rick Warren
Founding Pastor, Saddleback Church
Author, international bestseller *The Purpose-Driven Life*

A Note from the Authors

If you only had one month to live, what would you change?

This book is unique in many ways. Foremost, as the title and the question above demonstrate, we're not afraid to ask hard questions. As our first book, one we've waited more than ten years to write, these pages carry the vital message to which we're devoted—how to experience life to the fullest by living passionately and purposefully, the way we were created to live. By embracing the fact that our time on earth is limited, we can live deliberately, no longer postponing the joy and peace that come from fulfilling our God-given destiny. Unless there's nothing you want to change about your life, we look forward to exploring with you what it means to experience the one-month-to-live lifestyle.

This book is also unique because of the way we've written it. Both of us, Kerry and Chris, consider our lives and ministry to be an equal partnership. Married for over twenty years and ministering together for the entire time, we truly function better as a team. As we've struggled and stretched, grown and celebrated, we've lived the message in these pages. Therefore, about half the experiences and insights we share in these pages came from Kerry, the other half from Chris.

For your reading convenience, however, the book is written in one, first-person voice. This avoids the confusing shift between "I" (Kerry) and "I" (Chris) and eliminates an unnecessary distraction from the vital message we want to share. By combining our two voices into one, we also want to emphasize that our message transcends all demographics. It affects both men and women, singles and couples, rich and poor, and people of all cultures around the world.

Wherever you may be in your life's journey, we invite you to turn the page and begin answering this question that will forever change the way you live.

Kerry   *Chris*

THE ONE-MONTH-TO-LIVE

CHALLENGE

I commit with God's strength to live
the next thirty days as if they are my last
so I can experience life to the full!

Amanda Lyman Haney
Your name

[signature]
Partner's name

Kerry & Chris Shook

*Take the one-month-to-live challenge with a
friend and log on to OneMonthToLive.com for
daily encouragement from Kerry and Chris.*

ONE
MONTH
TO *live*

Introduction

LIVING THE DASH

> Death is more universal than life;
> everyone dies but not everyone lives.
> —ALAN SACHS

> I am convinced that it is not the fear of death,
> of our lives ending, that haunts our sleep so much
> as the fear…that as far as the world is concerned,
> we might as well never have lived.
> —HAROLD KUSHNER

*Y*our time on earth is limited.

No matter how much this idea makes you squirm, it's a fact. No matter who you are, how young or old, what measure of success you've attained, or where you live, mortality remains the great equalizer. With each tick of the clock, a moment of your life is behind you. Even as you read this paragraph, seconds passed that you can never regain. Your days are numbered, and each one that passes is gone forever.

If you're like me, you may be tempted to view this reality as harsh and unwelcome, to let it overwhelm and even paralyze you. But that's not my purpose in writing this book—just the opposite. I'm convinced that rather than inhibiting us to play it safe, *embracing our time on earth as a limited resource has incredible power to liberate us.* Most of us, if we knew we only had one month to live, would live differently. We would be more authentic about who we are and more deliberate about how we spent our time. But such a contrast begs the question: *what keeps us from living this way now?*

My motivation to find the answer—and better yet, to live it and help you live it—is born in part from my experience in ministry. In this role I've been privileged to spend time with many people as they face the imminent end of their lives on earth. While many of them struggle through the stages of grief—shock, denial, bargaining, guilt, anger, depression, acceptance—most of them make radical changes as a result of their awareness of their terminal conditions. They take license to say what they really feel and do what they really want. They ask for forgiveness and forgive others. They no longer think only of themselves but reach out to those they love and let them know how much they mean. They take risks they would never have taken before and allow themselves to lay worry aside and gratefully accept each new day. They seem to gain a new clarity about their priorities, like their relationship with God and leaving legacies that will endure.

Over the years of watching others live out their last days, I began to ask myself, *Why can't all of us live more like we're dying? Isn't that how we were meant to live in the first place? To discover what we're made for and to utilize our unique gifts in the limited amount of time we're given?* So last year at a staff retreat I tried a little experiment and asked our team members this question: If you knew you had one month to live, how would you live differently? I gave everyone a journal and challenged them to live the next thirty days as if they were their last and to write down what happened.

The results were nothing less than life changing! At the end of the thirty days, we all had a greater clarity of purpose and a renewed passion for the things that really matter. Many people did big, once-in-a-lifetime things, like going on a dream vacation to Hawaii with their spouse, finally getting serious about a healthy lifestyle and losing twenty-five pounds, or reconciling a relationship with a parent that had been neglected for years.

For me, the little, daily things took on a whole new meaning and forever changed my life. Taking my youngest two children to school every day became a real joy. I became keenly aware of what a sacred moment it is every morning to play twenty questions with Steven and to make up silly songs with my teenage daughter, Megan. I made sure that I met my two oldest sons, Ryan and Josh, at their favorite restaurant once a week after school just to connect. Many of our staff members did whatever it took to be at all their children's ball games, recitals, and school events. At the same time, I noticed that the team was more productive than ever, wanting the things they did at work to make a lasting impact.

I've since come to believe that the one-month-to-live lifestyle is universal in principle but unique in its expression. If we all lived as if we had one month left on this earth, we would each spend our days differently, in ways unique to us, and yet I believe we would all experience more fulfilling lives that could leave a legacy for eternity.

One Little Dash

Perhaps no place echoes with eternity quite like a cemetery. Not surprisingly, I'm fascinated by old gravestones and the lives they represent. The dates on some of the old monuments and grave markers in the Houston area where I live go back to the eighteen hundreds. My imagination launches me into the various stories the markers tell. I find myself pondering what life was like in 1823 or 1914. I know people back then had the same problems and pain as everyone does in life, but I wonder if they felt as stressed and pressured as I do. Our technology and modern conveniences have revolutionized our twenty-first-century lives but at what price?

Looking at old tombstones, I can't help but recognize that entire lives are now reduced before me to two dates and one little dash. Some monuments include facts or sayings, Bible verses or poignant memorials, but each person's life really comes down to what transpired between those two dates. It comes down to what's in the dash. I look at the dash of a particular person's marker and wonder, *What did he live for? Whom did she love? What were his passions? What were her biggest mistakes and greatest regrets?*

When you think about it, we don't have control over many things in life. We didn't get to decide where we were born, who our parents are, or which time period and culture we face. We don't get to decide the dates on our gravestone. We don't know when our time on this earth will be up. It could be next week or next year or decades away. Only God knows. Our lives are in His hands. But there is one thing we have a vast amount of control over. We get to decide how we're going to use our dash.

You get to choose how to spend that little dash of time between the two dates of your earthly existence. What are you spending yours on? Are you living the dash, knowing fully who you are and why you're here? Or dashing to live, hurriedly spending precious time chasing things that really don't matter to you? The psalmist prayed, "Teach us to number our days and recognize how few they are; help us to spend them as we should" (Psalm 90:12, TLB). God wants us to realize that our time on earth is limited so we will spend it wisely. But He gives us the choice about how we spend this most valuable currency.

No Change Required

While many of the people I've known who are facing death make radical changes in order to die well, occasionally I meet some who change very little. It's not that they are unwilling to change. It's that they have lived so deliberately and so authentically that the news of the end of this life doesn't turn them upside down. Of course they grieve and struggle with the news. They ache for their families and the people they love. But they take comfort in knowing they have been living focused on what matters most to them: their relationships with the ones they love, their relationship with the God of the universe, and the fulfillment of their unique purpose on this earth.

Wouldn't it be wonderful to spend your life so that if you discovered you only had a month to live, you wouldn't need to change a thing? What's holding you back? What are you waiting on? Repeatedly in Scripture, God reminds us that our lives are short compared to eternity. "Why, you do not even know what will happen tomorrow. What is your life? You are a mist that appears for a little while and then vanishes" (James 4:14).

Of course I'm not encouraging you simply to live for today. Most of us can't afford to quit our jobs overnight, say what we're really feeling all the time, or act on every spontaneous idea. This kind of a lifestyle seems selfish and wildly indulgent and may indicate that such a person doesn't believe there's anything beyond this life. But life is more than what we know of it on earth. Even as we engage ourselves in the present, we must think through the eternal impact of how we live. The Bible tells us that God has placed eternity in our hearts (Ecclesiastes 3:11). He created us in His own image as spiritual beings but in fleshly bodies. If we're honest, most of us sense there has to be more to our existence than what this world can offer.

This is the point where many people turn to faith. But just as some people live like there's no tomorrow, others use their faith to live like there's no today. They're always thinking about heaven "someday" instead of fully engaging in life today.

The only way we can live for eternity is to embrace each day as a gift from God. We must live in the tipping point between the everyday and the eternal. He created us and has given us another day to live—to know and experience His love, to love and serve those around us, to live passionately the life He made us for. The temporal nature of our lives should keep our focus on what matters most.

Thirty-Day Challenge

Be brutally honest with yourself. *Your time on earth is limited. Shouldn't you start making the most of it?* If you knew you had one month to live, you would look at everything from a different perspective. Many of the things you do now that seem so important would immediately become meaningless. You would have total clarity about what matters most, and you wouldn't hesitate to be spontaneous and risk your heart. You wouldn't wait until tomorrow to do what you need to do today. The way you lived that month would be the way you wished you had lived your whole life.

If you knew you had one month to live, your life would be radically transformed. But why do we wait until we're diagnosed with cancer or we lose a loved one to accept this knowledge and allow it to free us? Don't we want all that life has to offer? Don't we want to fulfill the purpose for which we were created? Wouldn't life be a lot more satisfying if we lived this way?

I'm challenging you to start living your life as though you have one month to live, and I've designed this book to help you. There are four universal principles in the one-month-to-live lifestyle: to live passionately, to love completely, to learn humbly, and to leave boldly. I've divided this book into four sections or "weeks" accordingly, and I encourage you to live these next thirty days as if they were your last. For each day there's a chapter designed to help you focus on that week's principle.

Each chapter also contains two features to inspire your thirty-day life experiment. Throughout each chapter, you'll find "Make It Count Moments" with questions designed to help you examine your life and focus on what's most important. The other feature, called "Make It Last for Life," comes at the end of each chapter and offers ways to act on that day's focus. These action points don't require homework so much as they inspire *lifework,* ways for you to personalize the material to your life. You may want to allow time to think through these items, to journal about them, and to pray about them. If you're reading this book with others in a group, then this will be a great place to focus your discussion.

Regardless of how you use this book, my hope and prayer is that you'll think seriously about what you want most out of life and what keeps you from pursuing it. I hope you'll embrace the fact that someday your life will come to an end so you will begin to live each day more fully.

You don't have to wait until there's a crisis to consider how you can experience life to the fullest. If you're willing to take this thirty-day challenge, be prepared for life to radically improve. You can live with no regrets and embrace a life so abundant you'll wonder why you ever settled for less.

There's no time like the present—right now!—to get started. Reading this book takes time, your most precious commodity, and I promise not to waste one second you spend on these pages. As you discover the life you were made for, today can truly be the first day of a life with no regrets. Claim today as the start of a month that's guaranteed to change your life!

Make It Last for Life

1. As quickly as possible, without thinking too hard or too long, make a list of five things you'd change about your life if you knew you only had a month to live. Choose at least one to begin changing today, right now.

2. Describe how you would like your life to be different at the end of reading this book. What drew you to open these pages in the first place? What's going on in your life now that has prepared you to think about who you are and why you're here?

3. Tell at least one other person—friend, family member, or co-worker—that you're reading this book. Ask that person to circle on the calendar the date for one month from today and to ask you then how your life has changed.

Live

Passionately

Roller Coaster

RIDING THE BIG DIPPER

Life isn't measured by the number of breaths we take,
but by the moments that take our breath away.
—ANONYMOUS

Somebody should tell us, right at the start of our lives,
that we are dying. Then we might live life to the limit,
every minute of every day. Do it, I say!
Whatever you want to do, do it now!
There are only so many tomorrows.
—POPE PAUL VI

As a kid, I loved going to the Spring Lake Amusement Park every summer—the smell of cotton candy, the carnival-type games with prizes, the Ferris wheel, and the bumper cars. But the main reason I loved the place was the roller coaster. To this day, the Big Dipper remains the scariest roller coaster I've ever ridden!

Now, I consider myself somewhat of a coaster connoisseur and have ridden several dozen, most of which I categorize as either "old-school model" or "new engineering feat." Sure, I like the sleek, state-of-the-art roller coasters with their steel tracks. They ramp up to new heights and reach breakneck speeds on the drop-off and turn loops and corkscrews and flip upside down. My kids love these, and we have a blast riding them.

The Big Dipper, however, was definitely old school and had none of the features of its modern counterparts. This baby was one of those old, wooden, traditional roller coasters, with slatted tracks and rickety scaffolding, chipped paint and cracked wood. No matter how jaded you might've been by other coasters, the Big Dipper guaranteed an adrenaline rush every ride.

As soon as the other thrill seekers and I boarded and left the station, I could feel my heart begin to race. We'd go up that first hill—*click, click, click, click*— until we got to the top, and then it would just stop, and I'd wonder, *Did it break? Are they going to come get us? What's going to happen here?* Then *BOOM!*—the bottom would drop out, and we'd take off, and my stomach would bounce into my throat. I had to close my eyes and mouth just to keep the bugs from flying in!

Hanging on for dear life, I felt so exhilarated and excited and genuinely afraid for my safety—all at the same time. We'd go around the first curve, and the wheels on one side would actually come off the track a little bit, and on the other side they would whine as sparks flew. Just as I got my bearings—*BOOM!*—another dip and another hairpin curve. I'd raise my hands to impress my friends, but, man, was I scared!

Even if I'd ridden it just the day before, I always felt disoriented enough to wonder what was next. The turns would keep coming so fast as my heart raced and my hands sweat on the little safety bar across my lap. We'd go into a tunnel so dark I could barely see the car in front of me and then out and into another curve and then—*SCREECH*—we'd slam to a stop back in the station.

Typical roller-coaster experience, right? Yet the Big Dipper's distinction, the unique feature that set it apart, was its age and visible lack of maintenance. It looked so bad that some of my friends wouldn't even ride it. Anyone could tell by looking, let alone riding, that it was just a matter of time before it jumped the track. OSHA hadn't inspected it in years! My friends and I had no idea if we'd be on the Dipper when it happened, but we definitely knew that one day it was going over the edge. In fact, years later a friend told me that once when he was riding it, the vacant seat next to him literally flew out of his car on the first curve!

Make It Count Moment

*Do you see your life more as a safe ride or a trip on the Big Dipper?
What areas of your life are safer than others? For example, maybe you
take huge risks to advance in your career, but you overly protect your
heart and risk little in relationships.*

Someday Syndrome

As I enter middle age, I'm convinced that my favorite roller-coaster ride serves as an analogy for the way we were made to live. With both, it seems we just get started, and then it's over. You knew it had to end sometime, but it just went by so quickly. It seems as though the longer you ride, the faster it goes. Both rides can be dizzying, disorienting, and exhilarating.

Just as the roller-coaster ride passes in a flash, our lives on this earth are temporal and finite. It's a natural part of being human; we're born, and eventually our bodies will die. Instead of finding this depressing or paralyzing, if you're willing to face and own this truth about life—that it will end as you know it here—then you can be truly free. Instead of limiting us, our mortality can consistently remind us to be all we were made to be.

Often we're tempted to play it safe and settle for far less than we were made for. I know so many people whose favorite day of the week is Someday. Countless people in every stage of life say, "Someday I'm going to go for all that life has to offer." "When I retire, then I'm going to enjoy life." "Someday I'm really going to live for God and get my act together. I'll start loving my family better." "When I make enough money, then I'm really going to spend more time with my kids." "Someday when my schedule slows down, then I'm going to get involved at church." "When I have more time, then I'll focus on being more spiritual."

Someday. One day. When. If. Then it's over. When are we going to wake up and realize *this is life*?

This is your life, right here, right now. Wherever you're reading this page, feeling whatever you're feeling, facing whatever you're experiencing, *Someday is right now.* We'll always be tempted to resort to the Someday Syndrome, but this mind-set robs us. Someday, when whatever we're looking for happens, then we'll start living. When everything settles down someday, then we can savor life. *But things won't settle down.* Once we attain what we think we want—more money, a less hectic schedule, the right job—we'll soon realize that it doesn't fulfill us, and we'll begin looking for the next big thing.

God did not design us simply to stand by and watch life pass as we wonder why we aren't more fulfilled. God created us to take risks in faith and to conquer the giants that paralyze us with fear.

We're to be like the teenage boy who stepped forward to challenge the giant Goliath in the ultimate death match. Despite all the thousands of men in the Israelite army, David was the only person who had the courage to face the giant. King Saul should have been the one to fight the Philistine giant, but he had long ago stopped following God with reckless abandon and was now playing it safe. Saul told David, "Don't be ridiculous! How can a kid like you fight with a man like him? You are only a boy and he has been in the army *since* he was a boy!" (1 Samuel 17:33, TLB).

When you think about it for a moment, you realize Saul was right in his assessment. What David was doing looked ridiculous! If you had been there, you would have said the same thing: "David, don't be ridiculous. Be reasonable. He's going to tear you apart limb by limb." Saul and the army of Israel were operating on the basis of reason. David was operating on the basis of faith. When you're operating on the basis of reason, all you can see is how big your giants are. If you're operating in faith, all you can see is how small your giants are compared to God.

The one thing that separated David from the thousands who were there that day was ridiculous faith. Let me humbly suggest that the only way you can slay the giants that stand between you and the life you were made for is "ridiculous faith." Saul and the army of Israel were looking at life from a ground-level perspective. When you look at life from the ground level, giants fill up the screen. David, on the other hand, was looking at life from a God-level perspective. When you look at life from His perspective, giants become really small. As I look at life from a God-level perspective, I begin to understand that the life of faith that everyone else calls ridiculous is the only reasonable way to live.

The world says, "Don't be ridiculous; be reasonable. Don't stand out. Don't take risks; play it safe, and make security and comfort your primary goals in life."

God calls us to a life of faith, living every moment all out for Him. God didn't create us to coast along on the "kiddie rides" as we called them at Spring Lake—those safe little rides that barely got our pulse up because they moved so slowly. He has promised us an abundant life if we'll get on board for the great adventure for which He designed us. Such a life of ridiculous faith is every bit as exciting as riding the Big Dipper!

Make It Count Moment

Are you doing anything in your life right now that requires faith? If not, why not? Are you looking at life from God's perspective or from a ground-level perspective?

God has set the track for you with clear guidelines, and He promises to be the ultimate engineer. He wants you to get on board and allow Him to take you to places you never dreamed you could go. Sometimes He goes at breakneck speeds so that your breath catches in your throat and you're holding on for dear life. You feel totally exhilarated and fulfilled and scared to death—all at the same time. *This* is what life is.

Life is unpredictable; you never know what's coming next. Sometimes you go around sharp turns and think the wheels are coming off, but God is an expert driver. He knows right where He's going, and He's in total control when you feel afraid. Sometimes you go into dark tunnels where you can barely see your hand in front of you, but that's when you feel His strong hand on your shoulder. Soon, though, you pull into the station, and the ride has ended. It seems as though the ride of life just gets started, and then it's over! If you've made the commitment to follow Jesus, however, the ride continues; God takes you with Him on to heaven for eternity.

Maybe this seems far removed from where you see yourself right now. Because of your life circumstances, you may feel like you've already jumped off the roller-coaster tracks and crashed on the pavement. As difficult and frightening as your life may be right now, God is still there. He cares about you beyond what you can understand or even imagine. If you knew you only had a month to live, wouldn't you want to leave the safe ride behind and get on the one that makes your heart come alive? Wouldn't you want to be on the ride that fulfills you—with joy, with fear, with a level of engagement that allows you to savor each moment? If you knew you only had a few weeks before this life ended, I don't think you'd be stuck in the Someday Syndrome. Today I want to challenge you to face your fears with ridiculous faith and experience the ride of your life!

Make It Last for Life

1. If you were certain your life as you know it would end in a few weeks, what would be your biggest regret? Why?

2. In what area of your life are you suffering from the Someday Syndrome? Make a decision today never again to use the phrase "someday, when things settle down." Realize that today is your someday!

3. Instead of a roller coaster, what symbol or metaphor would you choose to describe what your life would look like if you were fully engaged? Try to come up with something as unique as you are. Find a picture of that symbol, place it in a spot where you will see it every day, and use it as a reminder to live with no regrets. Go to www.OneMonthToLive.com for suggestions.

Time Squared

SPENDING YOUR MOST VALUABLE RESOURCE

> I don't want to get to the end of my life
> and find that I have just lived the length of it.
> I want to have lived the width of it as well.
> —DIANE ACKERMAN

> Guard well your spare moments. They are like uncut diamonds.
> Discard them and their value will never be known.
> Improve them and they will become
> the brightest gems in a useful life.
> —RALPH WALDO EMERSON

I once heard about a guy who went to the doctor to get the results of his annual physical. His doctor met with him and said, "I'm sorry, Bob. I've got some bad news for you. The tests show that you have a terminal disease. You only have six months to live." Bob let the news sink in and asked, "Is there anything I can do, any experimental drugs or treatment? There has to be something I can try." The doctor thought for a moment and said, "There is one thing. You can move to the country and buy a pig farm and raise pigs. Then you can find a widow who has fourteen or fifteen kids, marry her, and bring all of them to live with you on the pig farm." Bob looked puzzled and said, "And that will help me live longer?" The doctor said, "No, but it will seem like the longest six months of your life!"

You may groan at such a corny joke, but I think it illustrates a vital principle of our relationship with time. For some of you, the last six months have seemed like the longest six months of your life because you have no energy and no passion for life. Maybe you feel as if you're simply going through the motions, listless and discontent, wondering if this is all life has to offer.

Most of us have experienced seasons in our lives when time seemed to grind by as we watched the clock, willing the seconds to pass faster. On the other hand, you can probably recall times when the hours flew by. Think about those occasions when you lost all sense of time and felt entirely caught up in the present moment, immersed in the activity at hand or enjoying the people around you. What makes the difference? Why do some days feel so much more meaningful than others? How can we be fully engaged with the present and not get trapped by the past or paralyzed by the future?

To answer these questions, consider how you would view time differently if you knew your last day was just a calendar page away. If you knew you only had one month to live, certainly those remaining minutes, hours, and days would become your most precious commodity. Like a billionaire who suddenly discovers he's down to his last hundred dollars, you would immediately stop taking your time for granted and would be aware of how you spent every minute. You would want each of them to be rich with enjoyment, significance, and investment in others.

Time Squared

If their days were numbered, most people would want to spend their time carefully and deliberately. I haven't met anyone who knew their days were limited who wanted to catch up on television reruns and maybe spend a little more time reformatting their hard drive. It's not that these are bad pursuits. In fact, chores and mundane responsibilities are part of daily life. But if we knew we had one month to live, I suspect most of us would experience crystal clarity about how to prioritize our time. Certainly chores and duties have to be kept up on a daily basis, but even these can be connected to larger goals—communicating with our spouse, teaching our kids, or connecting with God. The mundane can become magnificent if we're plugged into each hour and each other.

Obviously, our priorities contribute powerfully to how we perceive time and how we spend it. We all have the same number of minutes in a day. There's nothing you or I can do to increase the length of a day to twenty-five hours, let alone the thirty or forty hours we might need in order to catch up. Bottom line, we're all stuck with twenty-four hours. How you invest those hours, however, can determine the difference between a sense of contentment, because you know you're doing exactly what you were made for, and a sense of regret. If you want to live with no regrets, then you may need to inventory your life and see how you've been spending your time.

Better yet, do a cost-benefit analysis of your time to determine if how you spend your days produces the benefits you desire. Jack Groppel, a peak-performance coach for many professional athletes, celebrities, and corporate CEOs, says time management is really energy management. I totally agree. You can experience the effect of multiplying your time by effectively managing how you apply your energy each day. If we appreciate our time as a precious gift to spend, then we're much more likely to be engaged and motivated to make it count.

It almost seems like a natural law of physics. When we increase our energy and level of engagement, we multiply our time. You can work eighteen-hour days and yet not be effective. In fact, it's probably detrimental overall, because you'll lose your creativity and health and eventually burn out. Most of us would agree that workaholism stems from poor energy management. In many ways it comes down to the contrast between quantity of life (how long you'll live) versus quality of life (how you'll live). I'm not talking about how to add years to your life but rather how to add life to your years.

Make It Count Moment

What consumes most of your time each day? Be as specific as possible in responding. Many of us might say work consumes most of our hours each day, but break it down. What exactly consumes you at work? How meaningful is it? How satisfying is it? How much of any given day do you spend doing only what you do best?

The Test of Time

Many of us, me included, waste so much of our time. How often do we hear and use the *b* word? *We're really busy.* Can you think of the last time you asked a friend how she was doing, and she said, "Great. Things are really moving slowly. I have plenty of time to get everything done and spend quality time with my family and friends"? We all work really hard. We have good intentions, and we have learned some habits and time-management techniques that bring limited improvements, but they leave little room for relationships. We get on the wave of success, but as it goes faster and faster, we just don't know how to stop it.

Time once spent cannot be reclaimed. Once an hour, minute, or moment is over, it's gone forever. However, we can redeem the remaining time we have. We can reconsider our God-given purpose and the eternal legacy we want to leave behind and allow them to guide our schedule moving forward. How do we refocus? The only way you and I can make the most of our remaining time is to spend each day in such a way that we leave behind a worthwhile legacy on this earth. In his letter to the church at Corinth, Paul wrote, "Companions as we are in this work with you, we beg you, please don't squander one bit of this marvelous life God has given us" (2 Corinthians 6:1, MSG). He was saying, "Don't squander your time because time is your life." If you waste your time, you waste your life. And if we're going to use our time in such a way that we leave a lasting mark on this earth, then we have to pass the effectiveness test.

Richard Koch, author of the best-selling business book *The 80/20 Principle,* studied many businesses and successful individuals and came to this conclusion: For most businesses, 20 percent of their activity produces 80 percent of their results. Twenty percent of their activity produces 80 percent of their profits. And he says the same thing is true for individuals. That is, 20 percent of what you do in your life produces 80 percent of your results. Twenty percent of what you do in your life produces 80 percent of your happiness. Twenty percent of the people you hang around with produce 80 percent of the joy in your relationships.

Basically, 20 percent of what you do brings about most of the results in your life, and 80 percent of what you do is pretty much wasted time. For example, a lot of people watch too much television. New studies even show that watching more than twenty hours a week can lead to mild depression. So it's not very productive, and it doesn't result in a lot of happiness, which makes it wasted time. If you spend more time in the areas that bring you the most results and less time in ineffective pursuits, then you will accomplish more by doing less!

Make It Count Moment

In general, do you agree with the 80/20 principle? Does it seem to fit your life and how you spend your time? What activities in your life would you consider wasted time? What keeps you from using that time in more meaningful ways?

Eternal Clocks

One of the challenges for most of us is what I call the productivity paradox. We're conditioned to believe that in order for our time to be worthwhile, we must have something to show for it. We produce something—another report, a new document, a better system, an improved product. Many people I know feel pressured to produce—even during their vacation and free time! They can't enjoy just relaxing by the pool or going for a walk or sleeping late, because they don't have anything to show for it.

The result is that we all need downtime to rest and to worship, to still ourselves before God, to think about our lives and to listen to His voice. The paradox is that we may not have anything to show for these truly productive moments. There is great freedom in learning to operate with an eternal perspective and not just by the watch on our wrist. A regular time of rest and recovery, a sabbath, is essential in our schedules. We need to become attuned to a greater measure of time than mere clocks and calendars.

If you knew you only had one month to live, wouldn't you want to take more time to linger over a meal with your family? to inhale the rich aroma of a cup of coffee as you watch the sunrise through your kitchen window? to cheer your son at his basketball game? to read a meaningful book, poem, or passage of Scripture? to take a walk through the piny woods, listening to the birds chatter?

None of these events will produce a product or allow you to point to an accomplishment. But they're essential to our well-being. I'd venture that most of your precious memories occurred in spontaneous moments when you were paying attention to the present. We're created for more than work. Our value is so much more than what we do.

In short, we're designed to require rest and to crave beauty. Even our Creator rested and observed a Sabbath. None of us would presume to be more productive than God, yet we often act as if we can't afford to stop, to pause, to still ourselves and rest at a soul level. If we're going to manage our time in such a way that maximizes it, then we must be willing to live by an eternal clock, listening to God in our lives as well as listening to our bodies and hearts.

If you're going to end the Someday Syndrome that we discussed in the last chapter, then you have to be willing to make "someday" happen today by listening and yielding to how you're made. Make the most of your time by applying your energy to the areas that are your ongoing priorities. Keep in mind the legacy you want to leave behind—in the work you do, through the relationships you keep, and by the way you spend each day. We were not designed to be slaves to time. We were created to be active and present in the lives we've been given. Make the most of your time by spending it on a legacy that will last long after your time on earth has ended. Do it today!

Make It Last for Life

1. Keep a time journal this week, and jot down how you spend each day. Try to rate your productivity (what you accomplish) along with your contentment (how you experienced each day). How would you rate the cost-effectiveness of how you invested your time?

2. What was the biggest time waster in your past week? What was the payoff for you? Did it distract you, entertain you, allow you to avoid someone? Is there a way to use your time differently and have a greater, more significant impact? Maybe you need to watch less television and to read more, or perhaps instead of surfing the Internet, you could go for a walk or get some other exercise. Come up

with a short list of alternate activities you can pursue the next time you're tempted to waste time by default.

3. How would you describe your current season of life? Does it feel like you're buried beneath frozen tundra, emotionally hibernating? Or is it more like spring, with signs of new life in view? What does it mean for you to accept and honor your current season?

Power Surge

CONNECTING WITH THE ULTIMATE SOURCE

> You don't have a soul. You are a Soul.
> You have a body.
> —C. S. LEWIS

> You formed us for yourself,
> and our hearts are restless till they find rest in you.
> —SAINT AUGUSTINE

During the many storms and hurricanes along the Gulf Coast, we often experience power surges that leave us wondering if we'll soon be scrambling for candles and flashlights. The lights flicker, all the electric appliances seem to sigh, and everyone in our home holds their breath to see what will happen next. Occasionally we're left in the dark for minutes, hours, or even days as the generators and power lines crash.

During these moments, when we're gathered in the kitchen lighting candles and looking for more batteries, we suddenly realize how dependent we are on power. To live the life we were made for, we're also completely dependent on power. We need the power to change. The problem is, we often think we can make the necessary changes with a little willpower, and we don't see how dependent we are on God's power.

People who know their lives will soon be over tend to feel a desperate urge to change. But a desperation to change is not enough. In order to sustain the changes, we have to be connected to a power source beyond ourselves—a power source that never wavers, flickers, or leaves us in the dark. We have to move from willpower to the real power that comes from a connection to our Creator. If you have come to the end of yourself and are exhausted from trying to control your life, Jesus offers you the invitation of a lifetime: "Are you tired? Worn out? Burned out on religion? Come to me. Get away with me and you'll recover your life. I'll show you how to take a real rest. Walk with me and work with me—watch how I do it. Learn the unforced rhythms of grace" (Matthew 11:28–29, MSG).

Make It Count Moment

In what area of your life are you struggling the most to change? Is it getting physically fit or losing weight? Is it breaking a bad habit? Is it a relationship issue? Are you trying to change with willpower or God's power? What words or phrases in Matthew 11:28–29 intrigue you? Why?

Spiritual Energy

While our lives include many facets, our spiritual energy is more important than the others, because everything else hinges on it. We're created as spiritual beings, and to develop spiritual energy, we have to cultivate a healthy connection to our Creator. The Bible consistently reveals that humans are created in God's image and that we have an eternal part of us, our spirits. The most important part of our lives is this spiritual dimension, our very souls.

We usually put a great deal of emphasis on physical health, and that's important, but many people completely neglect their spiritual health because they can't see it. Some people talk about spiritual growth and how they can stimulate it in their lives, but to gain the power to change, what we need to seek is not spiritual growth but spiritual health. Healthy things grow, so you don't need to focus on spiritual growth during this thirty-day challenge. Instead, focus on spiritual health.

If you only had one month left before your physical body collapsed, wouldn't you want the part of you that's going to live forever to be as healthy as possible? The key to spiritual health is maintaining a strong relationship with your Creator. If you are connected to your Creator, you will grow like you've never grown before, and you'll experience real power to make lasting changes.

Fruitful Living

How do we become spiritually healthy? Jesus tells us:

> I am the true vine, and My Father is the vinedresser. Every branch in Me that does not bear fruit He takes away; and every branch that bears fruit He prunes, that it may bear more fruit. You are already clean because of the word which I have spoken to you. Abide in Me, and I in you. As the branch cannot bear fruit of itself, unless it abides in the vine, neither can you, unless you abide in Me. I am the vine, you are the branches. He who abides in Me, and I in him, bears much fruit; for without Me you can do nothing. (John 15:1–5, NKJV)

In Christ's day, everyone understood what was required to produce the best possible crop of grapes. Vineyards were all around them, so Jesus' original audience knew exactly what He was describing. But we may not understand it quite as well, so let's examine it more closely.

First, Jesus says, "I am the true vine." In a vineyard, the vine is the source of energy, the lifeline that provides nutrients and produces the grapes. After the vine, Jesus describes the branches—us. If you're connected to the true vine, then you're a branch. And as much as we might not like it, branches by themselves cannot produce fruit. We're created to be connected to a larger power source. The branch bears the fruit, but without the vine, the branch can't produce it. Notice that Jesus says to the branches, "Abide in Me." To abide simply means to stay connected. If you want spiritual health, you have to stay connected to Christ, the vine. That's our job. That's all we have to do! If you want to reduce your stress, for this month and beyond, then realize your role in life is to stay connected to the vine.

Sometimes I forget my role, and I try to be the vine. I come up with a plan and a schedule, goals and an agenda. Then I try to work my plan and make everything happen according to the timetable I've set. Finally I get so stressed that I lose all my energy. I end up frustrated and exhausted and have nothing to show for my efforts. I forget that by itself the branch cannot produce life; it can only draw life from the vine. As strange as it may sound, it's not up to you to produce the results. You're not responsible for producing fruit; Jesus is. You don't have to sweat and strive, work harder, or discipline yourself to be more spiritual through sheer willpower. When you realize this truth, it's incredibly liberating!

Perennial Pruning

Any gardener or vintner knows that pruning is the key to producing the best fruit. After a little research, I discovered that in most vineyards today, the head gardeners train the pruners for two to three years before letting them cut the branches, because pruners can ruin an entire crop if they don't know what they're doing.

Our heavenly Father, the Master Gardener, is an expert pruner. He knows when to cut, where to cut, and how much to cut to produce the best in our lives. Often we ask Him to bless us and make our lives more fruitful—our families, our businesses, our finances. But rarely do we like the pruning process we must endure for our prayers to be answered. God prunes areas of our lives so we can bear more and better-quality fruit.

I'm guessing that some of you don't feel as if you're being blessed at this stage of your life. Most likely it's because you're in the middle of the pruning process. Despite how it may feel, this is good news. The pruning process is always painful, but it's always productive. You have a heavenly Father who knows what He's doing. He's an expert. He's pruning you right now so you'll bear more fruit. He wants you to fulfill the ultimate purpose for which He created you, to be as fruitful as possible.

All we have to do, our only role, is to be the branch and connect to the vine. If we are connected to the vine, we'll be spiritually healthy and be filled with His energy. Relying on Him will reduce our stress and allow us the freedom to be fully engaged in life. When we forget and start thinking we're the vine instead of the branch, we get stressed out, because that's a role we were never created to play.

The question then becomes, how can we stay connected to the vine? That's all you have to do this month! You don't have to work up enough willpower to quit smoking, you don't have to grit your teeth and will yourself to stay on that diet, and you don't need to figure out ways to fix your broken relationships. All you have to do is connect to the vine, the power source, and He'll give you, not willpower, but real power. He'll give you His power to do everything you need to do. We'll grow spiritually as never before as long as we remain connected to the vine.

Make It Count Moment

What are some ways you've seen God prune areas of your life? How have you handled the pruning? (Be honest—we all whine at times!) What has been the result of His cuts into your life? Where are you still waiting to see results?

Constant Connection

How do we maintain our connection to the ultimate power source? Just as nutrients, water, and sun are needed for the branches to produce plump, succulent grapes, we need two connectors to remain healthy, grow, and produce the best fruit. Constant *communication* is the first. A lot of people today, because of their high-tech communication devices, are constantly connected to their offices. What we need far more is to be constantly connected to God.

We maintain this connection through conversational prayer. When you wake up in the morning, it's vital to start your day right by just talking to God. Perhaps you look ahead and think about your concerns and expectations for the day. Maybe you're just grateful for the gift of another twenty-four hours and wonder how He would like you to spend them. As Hudson Taylor put it, don't have your concert first and tune your instruments afterward. Begin the day with God!

Then keep the conversation going throughout the rest of your day. You don't have to use a formal tone or stop everything you're doing. You don't have to talk to Him out loud, because God knows your thoughts before you even speak, so just honestly share your heart with Him. Talk to God all through the day about the problems you're facing, decisions that come up, and surprises for which you're grateful. When you feel angry and stressed out, talk to God about it. Dump it on Him. He can take it. All through the day you can be in conversational prayer with God to stay connected with Him.

The next element for a healthy spiritual connection is constant *confession*. This doesn't mean you have to seek out your pastor, priest, or minister and tell him the latest dirt on yourself. It also doesn't involve beating yourself up and feeling bad for a set period of time. No, it's really just another dimension of your ongoing conversation with God throughout the day. When you become aware of something you shouldn't have said or done, or something you didn't do but believe you should have, just confess it and move on.

We're all works in progress. We fail and succumb in weak moments to temptations, but we don't need to dwell on them and certainly not wallow in them. If we admit our failures and ask for His grace and forgiveness, God delights in cleaning our hearts and restoring our relationship with Him. It's a daily, moment-by-moment process. When you mess up, when you make a mistake, when you sin, just own it and tell Him about it. Confession simply means you take responsibility for failing and admit it to God rather than making excuses or comparing yourself to others you think are doing worse. Basically, you remind yourself that you can't do it on your own, that you need God and want Him to continue working in your life to provide you with the strength and power you need to thrive. Confession is agreeing with God that our way was wrong, and repentance is deciding to go God's way.

Communication and confession will keep us connected to the ultimate power source, the vine. This is the key for moving from willpower to real power. Resolutions and commitments are useless when we rely on our willpower. You may be able to keep them for a while, but eventually your own power won't be enough. You move from willpower to His power just by staying connected.

Make It Last for Life

1. What are the current barriers to spiritual health in your life? In other words, what keeps you from connecting to God as your primary source of spiritual life?

2. Write a letter or prayer to God, being as honest as you can about your present disappointments and frustrations. Consider how these problems or issues might be preparing you for a more fruitful season.

3. How are you doing in the areas of communication and confession? How would you practice them differently if you knew you only had one month to live?

Oxygen Mask

BREATHING FIRST

> This is your life.
> Are you who you want to be?
> —SWITCHFOOT

> In the event that our cabin pressure should change,
> an oxygen mask will be released
> from the overhead compartment.
> Please place the oxygen mask on yourself first
> before helping small children
> or others who may need assistance.
> AIRLINE SAFETY ANNOUNCEMENT

*D*epending on how frequently you fly, you may know this drill by heart. It's part of every flight attendant's monologue covering safety procedures at the beginning of a flight. The rationale for such instruction is obvious: you can't help anyone if you've passed out from lack of oxygen yourself.

However, these words also contain a powerful spiritual truth. If you're going to make the most of your time on earth, living a no-regrets lifestyle, then you need to engage fully with those around you. You want the people you love to know just how much they mean to you. You want to be a healing agent in the lives you touch, leaving behind a legacy with eternal impact. But the only way to accomplish these goals of authentic living is first to take time and focus on yourself. If you're not healthy spiritually, physically, emotionally, and relationally, how can you move beyond yourself and invest in others?

This truth is nothing new—self-help books, recovery groups, and inspirational sermons often contain this message. And maybe it's always hit you, like me, as a bit too self-centered, another excuse for self-absorption in a me-first culture. Like anything taken to an extreme, self-care can become a license to never grow beyond ourselves and our needs. But that's not what putting on the oxygen mask first is about.

In fact, loving ourselves is a biblical command. Jesus Himself said this in identifying the greatest commandments: "'Love the Lord your God with all your heart, soul, and mind.' This is the first and greatest commandment. The second most important is similar: 'Love your neighbor as much as you love yourself'" (Matthew 22:37–39, TLB). Most of us understand that we are to love God first and that we are to love our neighbor, but we miss the last part of this message: we are to love our neighbor *as much as we love ourselves.* Jesus indicates that before we can really love others and make a difference in their lives, we have to first love ourselves.

This message can certainly be used to justify selfishness, but the reality is just the opposite. You have to first take time to get healthy so you can impact the world around you. In fact, until you learn how to love yourself, you can never really learn to love and care for others the way God wants you to. You cannot teach someone else that which you haven't learned.

God wants us to cultivate energy spiritually, physically, emotionally, and relationally. We examined this spiritual connection in our last chapter. Our spiritual connection with God is like a limitless oxygen tank. Healthy bodies, emotions, and relationships emerge from putting on the oxygen mask so we can then help others. Let's look at the other three areas and consider what it means to "breathe first" as you care for your body, your emotions, and your relationships.

Get Physical

If you knew you only had one month to live, how would you treat your body? Would you stop forcing yourself to exercise? order extra fries in the drive-through? enjoy a bowl of ice cream every day? If your physical body only had thirty days left, it might be tempting to neglect it and go only for what feels good and tastes better. But how you treat your body is an area where the reality of the one-month-to-live lifestyle extends far beyond a few weeks.

Whether you have thirty days or thirty years left, you should realize that how you treat your body has a direct and lasting impact on the quality of life you enjoy. Giving up exercise, eating more desserts, and staying out late might seem great for a few days, but we've all experienced those slumps where our energy level plummeted because we neglected ourselves. Our bodies require sleep, exercise, clean air, water, and quality nourishment. If you want to feel good for longer than it takes for the ice cream to melt, then you must increase your physical energy. And in order to increase it, you must first focus on developing a healthy concept of your body.

How do you cultivate a healthy body concept? To answer this, we need to go back to the primary source of our oxygen—our spiritual connection with our Creator. If you're not connected to God's oxygen mask, then you're going to struggle with body image, because you're going to breathe in society's lies about what is acceptable. It's human nature to look around and compare yourself to others, but today's culture thrives on media and advertising that focuses on eternal youth, perpetual beauty, and lean, airbrushed bodies.

The Enemy of our success prefers that we breathe in the carbon monoxide he loves to feed us, messages such as "You can't be too thin," "Look younger at all costs," "Appearances define you," and so on. When we buy into these messages, we poison ourselves with wrong concepts about the true health of our physical bodies. To be healthy physically, we must be healthy spiritually and listen to what God says about our bodies. In a letter to the church at Corinth, Paul wrote, "Have you forgotten that your body is the temple of the Holy Spirit, who lives in you…, and that you are not the owner of your own body?" (1 Corinthians 6:19, Phillips).

I often see two extremes when it comes to the concepts people have about their bodies. The first is, some people worship the temple. They don't worship the One *in* the temple but the temple itself. These are the people who spend countless hours trying to look better. Each week they work out religiously at the gym and spend all kinds of money to improve their appearance. But here's the crucial problem: whenever you worship the temple, your body—something that's guaranteed to change—you'll feel insecure. The other extreme is just as harmful—

people who trash the temple. They neglect their bodies completely and couldn't care less about their overall health. Whether it's avoiding exercise, eating too much, smoking, or other harmful habits, disregard for your body's well-being adds up. It reduces both the quantity and quality of your life.

If you knew God was coming to your house for dinner tonight, wouldn't you want to pick up, clean, and prepare for His visit? You need to realize that God lives in your house right now. He lives in you. Your body is the temple of God, and that's why it's so important to take care of yourself and cultivate physical energy.

If you stay connected to the vine—it goes back to your spiritual health—then you move from willpower to God's power. Then He gives you the strength to exercise. He gives you the real power to stay on that diet. It's not that you'll become a vegetarian triathlete who prays throughout each meal, but you won't be caught up in worshiping or ignoring your body. You'll recognize it as God's creation that houses both your soul and His Spirit, and you'll put a priority on your physical health.

Make It Count Moment

What's the biggest physical challenge you face? Weight? Body image? Injury or disease? What would it look like for you to take better care of your temple? What one step can you take today toward improving your physical health? Check out our daily exercise and diet plan at www.OneMonthToLive.com. You'll find daily encouragement and practical tools to support your new, healthy lifestyle.

How Do You Feel?

The next crucial area where we must breathe first is in our emotional lives. So many people function according to how they feel. They work hard when they feel like it. They go to church when they feel like it. They act lovingly toward their wife or husband when they feel like it. They work at being a better parent when they want to feel better about themselves, not when their children need to feel loved.

A huge part of maturing, of growing up, is learning to acknowledge and experience our emotions without being controlled by them. It's certainly not like we can flip a switch and turn off our fear or push a button and be happy. We may not be able to control what we feel, but we definitely can control what we do with those emotions—how they affect our thoughts and behavior. Since our feelings can fluctuate based on our mood, circumstances, physical health, and other factors, it becomes essential that we go back to our primary source, our spiritual connection to God. As we endure the ups and downs of life, God's truth serves as an anchor point no matter what emotional storm we may be experiencing. The New Testament says, "For God gave us a spirit not of fear but of power and love and self-control" (2 Timothy 1:7, ESV). If I'm connected to my Creator with constant conversation and constant confession, then He'll give me the power and self-control I need.

It's important to realize that a healthy emotional life doesn't mean you stuff how you feel and hide your emotions. No, we are created as emotional beings. We just have to express our emotions without being controlled by them. Many of us are conditioned, directly or indirectly, to believe that showing our emotions is wrong, weak, feminine, and dangerous. In particular, some Christians believe they should never get angry, never be sad, never get too excited. It's important to get honest about your emotions. I'm not suggesting that you control your emotions by suppressing them. Denial and repression will wreak just as much chaos in your life as always acting on how you feel. One counselor friend told me that people who bury their emotions are trying to keep a beachball underwater. They can manage it for a little while, but eventually there's going to be a big splash, and that beachball's going to surface. On the other hand, don't let the course of your life be dictated by your emotions. Feel what you feel, but then do what God wants you to do.

Jesus experienced the full range of human emotions that any of us feel, yet He never sinned. Jesus got angry. Jesus cried. Jesus laughed. Clearly He experienced all the emotions we do, but He didn't allow them to control His thoughts, behavior, or interactions with others. He's our best example of how to feel all that rises up inside us and still yield to what God would have us do. It's obvious that Jesus faced some difficult emotions as His excruciating death approached—loneliness, uncertainty, fear, and apprehension. Yet He prayed that His Father's will would be done in His life.

Make It Count Moment

How do you usually handle powerful emotions? Do you tend to boil over or slowly simmer? Think of the last time a feeling overwhelmed you— fear, joy, disappointment, excitement, jealousy, or anger. How did you express it? What do you wish you'd done differently?

Relationally Connected

The whole reason we put the oxygen mask on ourselves first is so we can breathe in and get healthy and help someone else find God's oxygen. While relationships inherently include challenges, many of which we'll consider in our next section, they reflect one of the most significant aspects of how we're made. Just as God created us as eternal beings in temporal bodies, He designed us to live in concert with others. We were not meant to be self-sufficient and independent so that we can isolate ourselves and avoid other people.

If we knew we were facing only a few weeks to live, we would not want to die alone. We would want those we care about to know our truest selves, to know how grateful we are for them. We would want to give them our final heart messages. We would want to leave behind a relational legacy of enduring love and ongoing faith.

I hope everyone reading this book has so much longer—many healthy, wonderful years longer—than one month to live. But no matter how many calendar pages we turn in our lives, we must still realize just how short life is. We ask God to teach us to number our days and help us understand that time is limited so we can spend our time the way He wants us to. Only then can we fulfill the purpose for which He created us. Fulfilling our purpose as His creation, connected to God as our lifeline, allows us to get healthy physically, emotionally, and relationally. Breathing first is not selfish. It's essential.

Make It Last for Life

1. How would you rate your health in each of these four areas—spiritual, physical, emotional, relational—from one (terrible) to ten (fantastic)? What's the greatest challenge to improving your health in these areas? What can you do to work through this challenge?

2. Spend time journaling about a specific goal for each of these four areas that you can pursue during the rest of this month. Make sure the goals are *practical* and *measurable*.

3. Connect daily to www.OneMonthToLive.com and spend fifteen to thirty minutes working on your spiritual, physical, emotional, and relational health.

Monkey Bars

RISKING GREATNESS

> Security is mostly a superstition.
> It does not exist in nature,
> nor do the children of men as a whole experience it.
> Avoiding danger is no safer in the long run
> than outright exposure.
> Life is either a daring adventure
> or nothing.
> —HELEN KELLER

> A ship is safe in harbor,
> but that's not what ships are for.
> —WILLIAM SHEDD

When my son Josh was four or five years old, I took him to the park one day, and he immediately ran to his favorite spot. "Hold me up on the monkey bars," he said. So I lifted him up, and he grabbed the monkey bars, and I let go. His little shoes hung about five feet off the ground, and he was so proud, holding on all by himself with a huge smile on his face. After about a minute he got tired and said, "Okay, get me down."

I said, "Josh, just let go, and I'll catch you."

He got a worried look on his face and said, "No, get me down."

I said, "Well, Josh, if you just let go, I'll catch you."

"No, get me down."

"Josh, I love you. I promise, I'll catch you."

Some of you reading this may be wondering what kind of parent I am! Others may realize I was taking the opportunity for a teaching moment so Josh would know that he could trust me, that if he'd just let go, I'd be there for him. But that little guy held on with all his might. He held on until his knuckles turned white and he couldn't hold on any longer. Finally he let go, and I caught him.

A big smile came across his face, and I sat him down, and he ran off to play on the swings. He forgot all about it. But it struck me that God had a message for me in this scene, almost as if He was saying, *This is exactly the way you relate to Me. You hold on desperately, trying to do things in your own strength. You struggle endlessly, trying to control everything, trying to make everything just right, trying to please people, trying to control every situation. You hold on and think there's no one to catch you so you'd better grip harder and cling tighter. While you're hanging there and your knuckles are turning white, I'm saying, "Just let go, and I'll catch you. Just let go. I promise you, I love you, and I'll catch you."*

I work so hard to keep everything going the way I think it should go when God is right there all along. He says, *I made you with My own hands. I made you for a purpose, and I died to buy you back. Why can't you trust Me? I gave My life for you. I'm the God of the universe. You can just let go, and I'll catch you.* Why do I struggle with this so much? Each and every day I have to come to the place where I realize I can't control everything in my life, and I have to let go and surrender to God. He always catches me, and that's when I feel His peace and strength in the stressful moments of life.

Make It Count Moment

What are you clinging to right now that you need to let go of in order to move forward in your life? What keeps you from trusting that God will catch you?

Talent Show

The only way to risk greatness is to trust God with all areas of your life. Not only is it exhausting to hang on to the monkey bars so tightly, but it keeps us from pursuing the much larger and more fulfilling dreams God has for us. When we cling to our own goals and methods, we miss opportunities that would bless and strengthen us. God created us to take risks—not in a reckless "Vegas, here I come" style but in ways that are outside our comfort zones and beyond our own agendas. He wants us to trust Him to accomplish incredible things we could never achieve on our own. In fact, Jesus tells a parable that provides real insight into divine investment strategy.

He compares God's kingdom to a man who's leaving for an extended trip and therefore delegates financial responsibilities to his servants. "To one he gave five thousand dollars, to another two thousand, to a third one thousand, depending on their abilities. Then he left. Right off, the first servant went to work and doubled his master's investment. The second did the same. But the man with the single thousand dug a hole and carefully buried his master's money."

After he's been gone awhile, the man returns and calls in each of his three stewards to give an account of their resources. The first two associates reveal their success, and their boss is overjoyed. To each of them he says, "Good work! You did your job well. From now on be my partner." But then the third servant comes in and says, "Master, I know you have high standards and hate careless ways, that you demand the best and make no allowances for error. I was afraid I might disappoint you, so I found a good hiding place and secured your money. Here it is, safe and sound down to the last cent."

The master angrily declares, "That's a terrible way to live! It's criminal to live cautiously like that! If you knew I was after the best, why did you do less than the least? The least you could have done would have been to invest the sum with the bankers, where at least I would have gotten a little interest. Take the thousand and give it to the one who risked the most. And get rid of this 'play-it-safe' who won't go out on a limb. Throw him out into utter darkness" (Matthew 25:14–30, MSG).

The master's response to the third servant may sound harsh. However, ironically enough, this story reinforces the fact that God does not want us fearing Him in ways that inhibit our willingness to risk and grow. The third servant is so afraid of letting go of the monkey bars that he keeps hanging on. He doesn't trust the respect and love of his boss enough to believe his boss will catch him if he risks big and loses.

So often we play it safe, satisfied with the status quo and justifying our conservative approach by telling ourselves it's what God wants. But there's room to grow in virtually everyone's life. "From everyone who has been given much, much will be demanded; and from the one who has been entrusted with much, much more will be asked" (Luke 12:48).

Make It Count Moment

In which areas are you more likely to take a risk—personal, professional, relational, or spiritual? In which areas do you tend to play it safe? Why is it easier to take risks in some areas than others?

Risk Management

What keeps us clinging to our own efforts instead of risking the greatness that God directs us toward? For many of us, it's the loss of control. We think that if we really let go and allow God to catch and direct us, we'll end up spending our lives like a prison sentence, doing something we hate. But that couldn't be further from the truth! God has created each one of us to fulfill a purpose, and He has designed us uniquely to accomplish it. He's planted eternity in our hearts along with seeds of greatness that can only grow through our willingness to serve.

What does letting go look like? From my experience, it often involves patience and looking for God's hand in places we might not expect. God rarely conforms to our timetables or does things in a neat, linear way from our human and limited perspective. Sometimes we don't even realize what we were made to do, what really energizes and delights us, until we're forced into it, kicking and screaming. Writer and theologian C. S. Lewis said that too often we're like children who settle for playing in mud puddles when the beauty and immensity of the ocean are just a few feet away.

Our fear is probably the other huge obstacle that keeps us clinging to the monkey bars long after it's time to move on. And fear can certainly paralyze us;

we can easily become confined to a very narrow vision of our lives. It's almost as if we can't imagine how we could survive unless we get things the way we want them. Our perspective is limited and doesn't include possibilities that may seem improbable or even impossible when left to our own devices.

We've all heard stories about celebrities and successful businesspeople who failed miserably early in their careers, only to wander "accidentally" into new ventures for which they were naturally suited. Henry Ford wasn't a good businessman (he went bankrupt five times), but he was a visionary engineer. Oprah was fired from her job as a television reporter before launching her now-successful show and far-reaching media empire. In fact, if we looked at the lives of every person, both historical and contemporary, whom we consider "successful," we wouldn't find an absence of failure, fear, or pain. Instead we would find the common denominators of perseverance and purpose converging to motivate and inspire these achievers to move forward. They pushed through their fears, not only enduring failures, but learning from them.

The Bible tells us that perfect love casts out fear (1 John 4:18). It doesn't say that perfection casts out fear or that perfect love ensures our success the way we want it. When we know God's love, the care and compassion of a loving Father who wants us to trust Him, then we can let go. His love is so much greater than our fears. When one of my children fails a math test or fails to obey curfew, I don't stop loving him or her. And depending on the circumstances and why and how they failed, it can be an incredible teaching moment.

Similarly, God loves to redeem our failures, to transform our mistakes—whether rebellious or well intended—into part of His plan and our ultimate purpose. Look at David and Bathsheba—adultery, murder, denial, and finally confession and repentance. But God managed to turn an incredibly selfish, destructive mistake into something powerful and life giving. Bathsheba was the mother of Solomon, and he was in the lineage of David from which Jesus descended. She is even mentioned in the genealogy of Christ recorded at the beginning of Matthew's gospel (1:6).

Just Do It

One of the striking similarities among the people I've known who were nearing the end of their lives is the way they faced their fears and took risks. So often the things we put off only serve to keep our lives safe, comfortable, and mediocre. The difficult phone call to an estranged relative or loved one. The conversation with our children about what matters most. Asking forgiveness for something we regret doing or leaving undone. Acting spontaneously and living in the moment. Eating an ice-cream cone on a sunny spring afternoon.

We miss so many moments, large and small, when we aren't willing to break out of the pattern of least resistance and attempt greater things. But if we knew our days were numbered, and suddenly our priorities were clearly illuminated, it would make it much easier to hear God's call and take the plunge. We wouldn't be worried about what others think of us or what they would say. We wouldn't be worried about failing or wasting time, because we would recognize that regret would outweigh either of them.

If you're worn out from holding on so tightly and you feel as if you're losing your grip on life, let go of the monkey bars and feel the strong arms of a loving God catch you. In your heavenly Father's grip of grace, you'll experience the security and peace you've always longed for.

Make It Last for Life

1. Make a list of the items, resources, gifts, and opportunities you are presently entrusted with stewarding. Beside each one describe how it came to you (for instance, you were born with it, someone gave it to you, you worked for it), and then note how much control you had over how it came to you. Finally, jot down how you think God would like you to invest each item on your list and how you can pursue this investment.

2. When have you been disappointed by God? How did He not come through for you the way you wanted Him to? How did this affect your relationship with Him? How can you exercise trust in Him as your loving Father even when you feel disappointed? Spend some

time in prayer today relating your disappointment and asking Him
to help you trust Him more fully.

3. Write down one risk that you believe God is calling you to take
presently in your life. Describe your fears about taking this risk.
Describe the worst-case scenario if you take this risk and fail. Pray
that God will help you face your fears so you can do what He
wants.

Dreamsicle

THAWING OUT YOUR FROZEN DREAMS

> Our truest life is when we are in our dreams awake.
> —HENRY DAVID THOREAU

> There are people who put their dreams in a little box
> and say, "Yes, I've got dreams, of course I've got dreams."
> Then they put the box away and bring it out once in a while
> to look in it, and yep, they're still there.
> —ERMA BOMBECK

*O*ur dreams can be every bit as sweet and delicious as a Dreamsicle. Remember those? Orange sherbet wrapped around vanilla ice cream on a stick—man, I loved them as a kid! Fulfilling our dreams can be like chasing the ice-cream truck in the neighborhood, buying a Dreamsicle, and enjoying that cool, creamy sensation on a scorching day. A dream is something that calls to us, something that may seem impossible or crazy but tastes sweeter and more fulfilling than we ever could have imagined.

For most of us, though, fulfilling our dreams rarely goes smoothly. We end up feeling like our Dreamsicle melted too fast, fell off the stick, and landed—*splat*— on the sidewalk. Or maybe more accurately, we didn't lose our dreams. They're simply buried in the very back of our freezers, where they've become brittle, with freezer burn and ice crystals corroding their sweetness.

It doesn't take long for the blizzards of life to freeze our dreams. Everyday life has a way of wearing down the dreams of our youth and deflating the hope of seeing them come to pass. We get frostbitten by the bitter cold of disappointment, delay, and deferment. Instead of dreaming big and believing that God can accomplish great things through us, we go into survival mode and put our dreams on ice.

God has put us here for a reason and planted dreams within us so we can do our part in seeing them realized. Whether we have thirty days or thirty years, we want to leave this life on earth without regrets. "If only's" and "what-ifs" will haunt us unless we know that we poured ourselves into bringing our unique dreams to life. Many people, however, have no idea what their dreams are and what they really want in life. Don't you feel this way at times? Maybe when your job is getting you down and you wonder if you've completely missed your calling. Maybe when a relationship falls apart or when circumstances make you question if you're in the right place. Maybe when you're just bored and going through another mundane, daily routine. During these moments we tend to forget what our true desires and dreams are because they get buried under an avalanche of pain.

I believe God wants to thaw out that frozen dream that He placed in your heart. He wants to rescue you from an ordinary existence and bring your dream back to life! The Psalmist said, "Taste and see that the LORD is good" (Psalm 34:8). I have found there is nothing tastier and more fulfilling than discovering and following the dream God has planted in your heart.

Make It Count Moment

Currently how connected do you feel to your dreams? Does your day-to-day life reflect an active pursuit of your dreams? What prevents you from such a pursuit?

Dreams Float

Dreams come in more varieties than ice-cream flavors. But just because we want something and yearn to attain it doesn't mean it's the dream God planted in our hearts. So how do you know if a dream is really from God or if it's just an idea that popped into your head? For one thing, God's dream will never go against His Word, because His will never contradicts His Word. If the desire you have goes against God's Word, it's not His dream. Paul told us the secret to determining if a dream is from God when he said, "God…is able to do far more than we would ever dare to ask or even dream of—infinitely beyond our highest prayers, desires, thoughts, or hopes" (Ephesians 3:20, TLB). God's dream will rise to the top while everything else will melt away. Just as the ice cream in a root-beer float rises to the top, so does God's dream for us.

His dream rises to the top, first, because it requires faith. If a dream is from God, it will be so big in your life that you can't do it on your own. If you can accomplish it by yourself, no faith is required. The Bible says, "Without faith it is impossible to please God" (Hebrews 11:6). So if a dream is from God, it will rise to the top because it will be so big you can't do it alone. It'll have to be a God thing.

God's dream also rises to the top because it makes a difference in the lives of others. It's not a selfish dream. If you dream of making enormous amounts of money so you can retire early, live in luxury, and remove yourself from the cares of others, then it's clearly not God's dream. On the other hand, if you want to make a lot of money to give away, to serve His kingdom, to retire early so you can start a new career to which He's calling you, then it could be from God. Only you can know what His dream is for your life. God created us as social beings, just as relational as He is, and He wants us to love and serve others just as He does.

Another reason God's dream rises to the top is that it comes from your heart, from the core of your being. Whenever God gives you a dream, He places it deep in your heart. The word used in the New Testament for *heart* is most often *kardiva,* a Greek word that literally means "the real you." Scripture uses the word *heart* to mean your internal motivation, your love, and your passions. So when God gives you a dream, He places it in your heart. When God gives you a passion for something, He wants you to go for it because it's incorporated in your being, not because He's trying to hijack your life. He doesn't give you a passion for one dream and then call you to fulfill a life plan that's completely unrelated. That's not His character, nor is it good stewardship—and He never wastes the resources He's created.

Make It Count Moment

*How do you distinguish between your own selfish dreams and the
God-given dream planted in your life? How has God revealed and
reinforced His dream for your life? How have you typically responded
in the past? How would you respond differently if you only had one
month to live?*

Rocky Road

On the other hand, there is one who exists for no other reason than to play games
and deceive you. This enemy fears your heart, because he knows what God can do
through ordinary people like you to make an extraordinary difference in the
world. Satan knows the dream starts in your heart, so he's committed to wounding your heart, taking it out of action, and freezing your God-given dream with
soul-numbing cold. He constantly bombards you with messages that say you can't
do it, that you'll never amount to anything of substance. He wants our failures in
life to disable us and take us out of the dream hunt.

No wonder life is so hard. The Bible says God has a plan for our lives, an
intricately designed, grand plan. But Satan also has a plan for our lives. Nowhere
is the contrast between these conflicted purposes expressed more clearly than in
this passage: "The thief's purpose is to steal and kill and destroy. My purpose is
to give life in all its fullness" (John 10:10, NLT). God's purpose is to give you a
dream. Satan's purpose is to steal the dream. And you must understand how
relentless he is.

If he can't keep us from pursuing God's dreams for our lives, then he switches
tactics and tries to get us to doubt the dreams. One of his greatest allies is our
impatience, along with the fear, worry, anxiety, second-guessing, and frustration
that usually accompany it. We may pursue the dream and pour ourselves into its
fulfillment. We may do our part and wonder why God doesn't immediately
respond. But God is not a vending machine, and His timing usually differs from
our expectations. If the examples from Scripture and our own experiences today
are indications, there will be a waiting period before the dream materializes.

We'll experience a detour, an indirect route on the road to seeing our dreams become reality.

In this waiting period we start asking questions like "When is this ever going to happen? *Is* this ever going to happen?" "When, Lord, am I ever going to get married?" "When, Lord, am I ever going to get over this hurt?" "When, Lord, am I ever going to get through this problem?" "When, Lord, are we ever going to have a child?" "When, Lord?" If you are in the waiting room of life right now, you are not alone.

Abraham was told by God that he would be the father of a great nation. He was ninety-nine before he had a child! Moses became the leader to guide the Jewish people out of slavery in Egypt—their plight for over four hundred years— but first God sent him to the desert to tend sheep for forty years. Even Jesus Christ, the Savior of the world, waited thirty years before He began His ministry on earth.

Why does God send everyone through the waiting room of life? I believe it's because He wants us to learn to rely on Him. God is preparing us to fulfill the dream by teaching us to trust Him. While we're waiting, we learn that He is right there with us and promises that "never will I leave you; never will I forsake you" (Hebrews 13:5). We may not understand what God is doing at the time, but we can always trust His heart.

When life gets hard, when we're hurting and weary, we must remember what's at stake. When we are wounded, we're tempted to bury our dreams deep in our heart, where they freeze over. All the wounds from our past can keep us from believing that God could ever use us. We fail so many times. We're such a mess. We're so weak and tired. We want to give up the dream, fearing it's too late.

But with God, it's *never* too late.

The incredible irony is that God delights in healing our wounds and turning them into strengths to accomplish the dreams He has for us. God can take the very painful experiences that you would like to forget and use them to make a difference in the lives of others. In the Bible, Joseph's brothers sold him into slavery—the Enemy stealing the dream. God used the circumstances to bring Joseph into power in Egypt during a famine—fulfilling the dream. Always remember that no matter what you're going through, no problem can destroy God's dream for your life!

Make It Last for Life

1. Pull out your "dream box." What's in there? What are *your* frozen dreams? In other words, what would you attempt for God if you knew you couldn't fail?

2. Write out a description of one dream you have that you believe is from God. How has it "floated to the top" in your life? How does it require faith on your part for it to be realized? How does it serve others?

3. Spend time in prayer, asking God to reveal one thing you can do today to further your pursuit of His dream for your life.

Kick Start

LIVING LIFE FULL THROTTLE

> Don't ask what the world needs.
> Ask what makes you come alive, and go do it.
> Because what the world needs
> is people who have come alive.
> —HOWARD THURMAN

> It is never too late to be what you might have been.
> —GEORGE ELIOT

Do you ever feel powerless in life? Many people tell me that the number one reason they don't try to change is because they feel powerless to alter the combined force of all the circumstances in their lives. Maybe you have a habit you feel powerless to break. Or maybe you have a problem in a relationship, and you've tried everything to restore it, yet it's still falling apart. Or maybe an issue at work is draining your energy and your creativity, and you can't see a solution. It could be that your schedule is overloaded, your in-box is overflowing, and you feel completely overwhelmed and burned out. Your emotional batteries are drained, and your mental energy has evaporated. You're not alone; at times we all feel powerless.

Recently my family and I went to a motocross track and were amazed at all the bumps and turns, curves and switchbacks packed into the rolling hillside before us. As our turn to ride approached, we were instructed on how to control our bikes—with 250 cc, they pack a big engine with a lot of power.

Then it occurred to me: what if I just *pushed* my motorcycle around the motocross track? Suppose I never kick-started the engine, never tapped into the engine's power, but just pushed the bike around the track and over the hills and around the sharp curves. That would be crazy, wouldn't it? Yet this is the way so many of us face life. A critical transformation takes place when we realize we have all God's power available to us. His limitless store of strength provides the oomph we need to power our lives. We have God's horsepower to help us, to heal our marriages, to restore our finances, to save our families, to intervene in our workplaces, and to rescue our lives. His power is available to help us live the lives for which He created us, but so much of the time we live in our own strength. We try to climb the hills and tackle problems without adequate power to finish the course.

People facing the end of their lives are forced to recognize their powerlessness and limitations. The weaker they get, the more they have to depend on others to take care of them. At the end of the day, they know that much of their lives is out of their control. Ultimately, they're forced to turn to God. The ironic thing is that when they finally stop struggling and rely on His strength, they discover real power to live the rest of their lives to the fullest.

You have the same limitless power available to you each and every day. Do you feel like you've been pushing a motocross bike around a rugged track? With a powerful engine, all you have to do is kick-start it and tap into God's power for your life. In Ephesians, Paul says, "I pray that you will begin to understand how incredibly great his power is to help those who believe him. It is that same mighty power that raised Christ from the dead" (1:19–20, TLB). He'll give you all the power you need for the one-month-to-live lifestyle.

High-Side Crash

Life bears many similarities to motocross. Tough turns and sharp curves. Jagged ruts and deep grooves. A smooth stretch but then watch out—another turn. In motocross the bumps and hills are called *whoops*—how great is that? These are just the normal jolts and scrapes, the bumps and bruises to be expected as part of the fun. And then there are crashes.

When a motocross rider goes into a turn and leans in too far and crashes, it's called a low-side crash. But when a rider goes into a turn, then flips—the turn flicks him to the outside—it's called a high-side crash. And a high-side crash is usually much more violent because of the leverage and increased G force. These crashes can be life threatening and career ending.

At times we all crash on the track of life. It's not a matter of if we fail but when we fail. It's just part of life. Everyone who has succeeded has also failed many times. While struggling to invent an electrical light, Thomas Alva Edison declared, "I have not failed. I've just found ten thousand ways that don't work." We need that same persistence to keep going. The greatest power we need in our lives is the power to begin again. So how do you start over after a crash? How do you move out of the starting gate and get a fresh start in life after you have failed?

My favorite example of someone rebounding from a high-side crash is one of Jesus' apostles, Simon Peter. As far as crashes go, he totally wiped out! Yet God gave him the power to begin again. Peter became a great champion for Christ, one of the greatest of all time, and the foundation of the church. If we reconstruct Peter's crash site, three lessons emerge that are as relevant for us as they were for him. When life's forces hit us hard and we crash and burn, it's great to know that God is the God of second chances, and He wants to give us the power to begin again. It's not just the power for a fresh start; it's also the power to get back on the track and go faster than ever before.

Make It Count Moment

When was the last time you experienced a high-side crash? How did you handle it? How has its impact continued to influence your life? your relationships with those you love? your relationship with God?

Loss Lessons

If you're going to have the power to begin again, you must learn from your losses. The key to not only knowing this lesson but owning and activating it is to humbly admit our failures. Peter was one of the original members of Christ's racing team. In fact, Jesus changed his name from Simon to Peter, which means "the rock." And Jesus said, "You're going to be the team captain, my anchor man, my foundation. I'm going to build the whole team around you. You're the rock. You're a champion, Peter" (see Matthew 16:17–18).

Just as we're prone to do, Peter became overconfident. On the night that Jesus gathered the team in the upper room, the night before the big race, He warned them, "This is going to be the most difficult race of your lives. The track conditions will be the most difficult you've ever experienced. This is like nothing you've ever faced before. The jumps are higher, the turns are sharper, and before it's over, every one of you is going to crash."

But Peter said, "Not me, Lord. Don't you remember? I'm the rock. I'm the champion. I'm not going to crash. You can count on me. I'll be with You at the finish line. I don't care how high the jumps are. I don't care how sharp the curves are. I don't care what condition the track is in. You can count on me. I'm going to be right there with You till the end" (see Matthew 26:31–33).

But then what happened? Right out of the starting gate, Peter crashed. And it was a high-side crash. I mean, it was a bad one. He didn't just fail his friend— Peter denied that he even knew Him. He became afraid, lost his nerve, and denied Jesus three times. And it got worse. There was a special spectator in the stands: "The Lord turned and looked straight at Peter. Then Peter remembered the word the Lord had spoken to him: 'Before the rooster crows today, you will disown me three times.' And he went outside and wept bitterly" (Luke 22:61–62).

Jesus didn't have to say a word to Peter. He just looked at him, and Peter remembered how he had bragged about his loyalty just hours before. Jesus looked right into Peter's heart and saw the regret, the guilt, the shame. He didn't condemn His friend or yell out, "I told you so!" as I might be inclined to do. He looked at him with compassion and didn't speak a word.

Just like Peter, some of you are in the middle of a crash site. Maybe it's a crash in your marriage, a crash with your kids or even your parents, a crash in your business, or an emotional crash. And Jesus doesn't have to say a word to you. He just looks with compassion right into your heart. He sees the guilt and the regret and the shame. But He does say something to you. He says that because of the power of His love for you, failure is never final. Because of the power of the Cross—the ultimate sacrifice producing power over death—our weaknesses and failures and selfishness can never keep us down. Failure is never fatal. We have the God of the second chance, and He wants to give us the power to begin again.

I have to admit my sins so I can be forgiven. I have to admit my failures so I can learn from them. "A man who refuses to admit his mistakes can never be successful. But if he confesses and forsakes them, he gets another chance" (Proverbs 28:13, TLB). When we admit our mess-ups, we get another chance. When we take responsibility for our failures and don't blame other people, God forgives and gives us the power to start over.

There's more: you must also release your guilt. Let it go! After a rider crashes, it's important for him to get back on the bike as soon as possible to overcome his fears. It's the motocross way of getting back on the horse. You may feel like you're so far off God's track for your life right now that you can never get back. You've made a lot of mistakes, a lot of selfish choices. You've let down a lot of people. You feel like your race has ended in a messy crash.

I have news for you: get ready for an amazing race. God says, "I still have a race for you to run!" Look what the angel said after Christ rose from the dead: "But go, tell his disciples and Peter, 'He is going ahead of you into Galilee'" (Mark 16:7). The angel said, "He's alive. He's not here. You need to go tell the disciples He's alive, and, oh, don't forget Peter. Remember, Peter is still included. He's still one of the disciples. Don't forget Peter."

Jesus knew that Peter was totally broken and thought God could never use him again. He believed he had completely blown it and the race was over for him. Christ wanted him to know, "Peter, I still have a race for you to run. I know how you're feeling, but you're still included. I still have a plan for your life. I'm going to give you the power to begin again, to become a great champion for Me." God says the same thing to you today: "I haven't forgotten you. I have a great race for you to run. Get up and let's go!"

Make It Count Moment

What's the hardest lesson you've learned from one of your life crashes?
How has learning that lesson strengthened your character? your faith?

Power of Denial

After learning from his losses and releasing his guilt, Peter's next step was to surrender to God's strength. It's almost as if Peter realized he'd been using the wrong fuel—one that contributed to his engine trouble and spectacular crash. Like Peter, to begin again we need to surrender to God's power. But surrender means yielding—giving ourselves over to His way of doing things. Jesus explained it this way: "If anyone would come after me, he must deny himself and take up his cross daily and follow me" (Luke 9:23). Jesus tells us to deny ourselves in order to find fulfillment. I have to choose to give up my way and follow God's plan and purpose for my life if I'm truly going to be fulfilled and live in the cross hairs of the abundant life He promised me.

This is just the opposite of what we hear every day in the world around us. We have to exchange mantras—from *satisfy* myself to *deny* myself. Peter denied Christ, and he crashed. But when he learned to deny himself, he became a champion. Can you relate? Every single day of my life, I come to the place where I realize I can't do it. I come to the place where I say I want to engage with my kids, but I feel worn out. I feel selfish. I want to be a better marriage partner, but I don't have the love I need. I want to make a difference at work, but I don't have any energy. Every day of my life, I come to the place where I fall on my face and say, "God, I can't do it. I give up." And God says, *Finally. I've been waiting for that. Now I can get involved and give you My power and My strength.*

When we give ourselves to God as the source of all the power in our lives, then we see results we could never attain on our own. Never. No matter how hard we tried. We will fail repeatedly at our attempts to change if we're only doing it for ourselves, by ourselves. God has so many more resources available to us—limitless fuel on an incredible track we can't even imagine. It's the plan God has for you, the race He's laid out for you. You were designed to go full throttle!

Make It Last for Life

1. Make a list of all the things you can think of that prevent you from fully trusting God with your life: past disappointments and hurts,

losses, doubts, and so on. After you finish, ask yourself what it would take for you to trust that somehow God can use each of them to fulfill His purpose in who He made you to be. Spend a minute in prayer for each item, and ask for help in releasing it.

2. What's your greatest fear about trusting God completely with your life? What's the basis for this fear? Journal about how you would face this fear if you only had one month to live.

3. When we've failed and are trying to get back on track, it's often helpful to talk it out with a person we trust. Call someone today and make a plan to get together over coffee to share where you are on your faith track.

Love Completely

Heart of the Matter

RELATING AND NOT WAITING

> Vanity it is,
> to wish to live long,
> and to be careless to live well.
> —THOMAS À KEMPIS

> The measure of a life, after all,
> is not its duration
> but its donation.
> —CORRIE TEN BOOM

*W*hen all is said and done, relationships are all that really matter. It doesn't matter how much money we have, where we live, or how many beautiful toys we've collected. None of these can comfort us, console us, cry with us, or love us. Our investment in the people we care about is the only legacy that has the power to endure beyond our lifetime.

As we shift into our second section and focus on loving completely, we'll be examining the impact the one-month-to-live lifestyle can have on our relationship with God as well as others. God designed us to be in relationship both vertically with Him and horizontally with the people around us. Even though we may have a deep desire to connect with our families, friends, and communities, we've all experienced some of the messiness of relating to others. Expectations, disappointments, betrayals, hurts, lies, misunderstandings—there are so many obstacles to loving other people and being loved by them. But we were created for relationships, and if we only had one month left, we would be more concerned about them than ever before.

If you've ever lost a loved one, you know how important it is to try to wrap up any unfinished business between you. It can be as simple as expressing how much you love each other or as complicated as discussing the impact of a lifetime of failures and then asking forgiveness. Either way, both of you consider it a priority—rearranging schedules if necessary, traveling great distances, and speaking from your hearts.

If you were the one whose time was short, you would want to connect with those people in your life whom you value most. You would want to give them the gift of time together, to say all that you want to say, and to allow them to know the real you. You would want to leave them with memories, words, and a personal investment that would linger long after you're gone.

Today, though, most of us are so busy, constantly in motion, that maintaining close relationships—even with our spouses and immediate families—proves challenging. We work long hours to provide for the people we love, to give them luxuries and benefits we may not have experienced ourselves, but we miss spending quality time with them. We can give them expensive gifts and vacations, but we struggle to give them our time and undivided attention.

So why don't we live as if our relationships matter most? Why do we wait until people are dead to give them flowers? It seems ironic that most of us value relationships but don't expend the energy to invest in them fully. In hyperspeed hustle of our overscheduled lives, many of us tend to take others for granted. A spouse can become just another supporting player, a roommate who helps with the finances. Our children turn into people who burden our schedules when they need us to take them to school, soccer practice, or the mall. Family get-togethers become social obligations, like the company Christmas party. But if we only had one month to live, suddenly we would realize just how much we need other people as well as how much they need us.

Make It Count Moment

If you only had a month to live, whom would you want to spend the time with? Whom would you need to apologize to? Who needs to be assured today that you love them? What keeps you from spending the time and saying these words now?

Social Studies

If much of our lifetime is still potentially before us, it's tempting to take the people in our lives for granted. We want to protect our hearts from the messy business of relating and detach ourselves from what's going on below the surface. We become strong and independent, relying on no one but ourselves. The only problem is that no matter how much we may try to isolate and insulate ourselves from others, this goes against our fundamental nature. Sure, some people are extroverts and some introverts. But all of us are designed as relational beings, social creatures who yearn to belong. It's the way God made us—in His image.

Two core truths of human existence can be found in the first book of the Bible. In the story of God's creation of man and woman, we see that we need more than just ourselves, apparently even more than just our relationship with God. "The LORD God said, 'It is not good for the man to be alone. I will make a helper suitable for him'" (Genesis 2:18). So God provided Eve to join Adam in the garden.

You know the rest of the story—the forbidden fruit, the serpent's seduction, the banishment from the garden. And what seems the most striking of all—Adam and Eve were in it together. "When the woman saw that the fruit of the tree was good for food and pleasing to the eye, and also desirable for gaining wisdom, she took some and ate it. She also gave some to her husband, who was with her, and he ate it" (Genesis 3:6). They were partners in crime, and by choosing to disobey God, they opened the door to sin and were never the same. They became parents of the human condition—the selfish nature that all of us inherit. Like Adam and Eve, we want to be like God and have it our way. Their turning point in the garden planted the seeds of strife, and relationships have never been the same since.

Make It Count Moment

Who in your life has disappointed you most? How have you handled that
relationship—blame, distance, denial, forgiveness? Some other way?
How have the pain and disappointment affected your other relationships?

The Price of Love

So we're designed for social and emotional intimacy with those around us, but our desires are polluted by our selfish inclination to make it all about us. Basically these two forces remain in conflict for the duration of our lives. We want to love other people, to be known and enjoyed and loved in return. But people disappoint us, hurt us, and don't usually respond the way we want them to. So we settle for playing it safe, telling ourselves that we don't really need them after all, but our hearts tell us otherwise. Mother Teresa said that loneliness is the most terrible poverty. She was right—without love we're emotionally bankrupt.

Love can't be bought, but it definitely carries a price, and it's called sacrifice. Love always means risking pain. Even in the best relationships, there's a haunting sense of potential loss—if nothing else, the possibility that the other person will die someday, leaving us alone. We love someone, get married, and then discover how painful an all-out intimate relationship can be. Many of you have experienced the incredible grief of losing parents. Children you invested your life in grow up and eventually move away. Our closest friends change jobs and relocate across the country. We don't stop loving any of these people, but we ache because we can't be with them and can't remain connected to them the way we would like. Pain is an inherent part of any significant relationship.

If we're going to love other people, to endure the heartaches as well as to celebrate the sharing of lives, then we will need a greater love than our own. We need to experience the fullness of God's love for us in order to die to our selfish desires and give freely to others. We have to look to God first. As much as we're made to need others, people can never fill our ache to be loved the way God can. He demonstrated His love in a way that forever changed history and continues to change countless lives today.

The greatest sacrifice of love in history occurred in Christ's death on the cross. God allowed His only Son to become mortal—Word made flesh—and then to endure the most excruciatingly painful and publicly humiliating death possible: crucifixion. God's love for us is truly incomprehensible. Our love has limits, but God's love has none. It's completely unconditional, no strings attached.

God's sacrifice reminds me of the story of a man who operated a drawbridge over a bay in a small ocean town. Every day he would walk up to the office next to the drawbridge, where he could control the lever. He would pull up the lever, the drawbridge with the train track on it would rise, and enormous ships would glide through. Then he would push the lever down, and the drawbridge would lower so the train could cross safely.

Almost every day his little boy would go to work with him—he loved to watch his dad raise and lower the drawbridge. One day when they were there together, the dad was radioed that a nonscheduled train was on its way and he needed to lower the drawbridge. He glanced out the window just as he was touching the lever, and he saw his little boy outside playing in the huge gears of the drawbridge next to the shore. He yelled for him, but his son couldn't hear him with all the commotion and noise near the water.

The man raced out of the office and ran toward his son to try to grab him and pull him to safety, but then the horrible truth struck him. If he didn't push down that lever right away, the train would plunge into the sea, and hundreds of passengers would die. But if he lowered the bridge, his son would be killed. At the last possible second he made his terrible decision, raced back to his station, and pulled down the lever, falling to his knees in agony as his little boy was crushed to death. With tears streaming down his cheeks, he looked out and saw the train racing safely over the bridge. He could see in the window of one of the dining cars that people were eating, drinking, and laughing, totally oblivious to the great sacrifice he had just made so they could live.

Most of us are totally oblivious to the great sacrifice God has made. He gave His only Son, who came to this earth and died for us to forgive us of our past guilt, to give us purpose in the present, and to give us a future that includes heaven. As you think about what it means to give sacrificially to those around you, maybe you should first think about how much God has sacrificed for you. My prayer for everyone reading this is the same as the one Paul expressed in his letter to the church at Ephesus: "And I pray that you, firmly fixed in love yourselves, may be able to grasp…how wide and deep and long and high is the love of Christ—and to know for yourselves that love so far beyond comprehension" (Ephesians 3:17–19, Phillips).

Your problem is not that you don't love God enough. It's that you don't understand how much He loves you. If you could grasp just a little bit of how much God loves you, you'd surrender all areas of your life to Him. God would have given up His Son to come to this earth and die on the cross if you had been the only one on this earth. If you were the only passenger on that unscheduled train, He would still lower the drawbridge—at the expense of His only Child—to cross the gulf between you and Him. He loves you that much.

With His love as your foundation, you can discover a new power in the way you relate to others. You can be free to be yourself, not looking to them for validation, approval, or permission. At the same time, you will relieve them of the pressure of having to mean more to you than is humanly possible. If you cut through the busyness and blurred priorities and absorb the fact that your remaining time on earth is limited, you can experience more intimacy in your life than ever before.

Make It Last for Life

1. Make a list of the people you would want to see and to share your heart with if you knew your time on earth was limited to one more month. What specific steps could you take to connect with one of them and share your heart? It could be as simple as making a date with your spouse or planning a reunion with a close friend.

2. Choose someone you know you have hurt by your words, actions, or silence. Write a letter asking this person's forgiveness and explaining everything you'd like to say before it's too late. Set the letter aside for a few days, and then reread it and decide if you should send it.

3. Think through your schedule for the next day or two. No matter how busy you may be, find a time to surprise someone you love. Take a friend to a favorite restaurant. Pick up the kids early from school and go to the park. Kidnap your spouse from the office and go out for coffee. Find a way to add quality connections to your life on a daily basis.

Ocean

EXPLORING THE DEPTHS OF FORGIVENESS

> He who cannot forgive others
> destroys the bridge over which he himself must pass.
> —GEORGE HERBERT

> He who is devoid of the power to forgive
> is devoid of the power to love.
> —MARTIN LUTHER KING JR.

When I go to the beach, I notice that many people flock to the shore but never get in the water. They just lie on their blankets and bake, keeping dermatologists in business. Others get in the ocean and splash around a little, maybe up to their waists, but never venture far from shore. Some people explore a little more seriously. They put on a mask and fins and snorkel around and appear to go deeper. But they're still only on the surface.

My family and I love to scuba-dive, and a few years ago we all earned our divers' certificates. Whether it's shipwrecks or sharks (well, maybe not the sharks for me!), we love to explore this underwater world that covers more than two-thirds of the earth's surface. I quickly learned that a scuba diver can go down safely only about 130 feet. At first this sounds deep, but think about it. The deepest place in the ocean is the Mariana Trench, at more than 36,000 feet. It's almost seven miles deep, and we can go down only 130 feet! Even if we use submersibles, most of the ocean is too deep and vast to be explored.

God's love is the same. Usually we just splash around on the surface, but He offers us a whole other level of depth in life. If we only had one month to live, I bet most of us would finally venture into deeper water, realizing that the only way we can be at peace is to confess our sins and experience the forgiveness and mercy He so freely gives.

Our sins, faults, and failures don't go away—we either confess or suppress. In the rut of our busy everyday lives, it's easy to keep suppressing our mistakes, clinging to denial. But if the end was in sight, we would realize that we couldn't wait any longer. The key to how we leave this earth basically comes down to how we experience forgiveness and extend it to those around us.

Make It Count Moment

If you only had one month to live, what would you ask forgiveness for? From whom? Whom would you need to forgive?

Beneath the Surface

A deep-sea diver in a specially designed compression suit can go down much deeper—around a thousand feet—than I can in my wetsuit and scuba gear. The Lord's Prayer functions the same way; it allows us to go much deeper and to get to the heart of what matters most: forgiveness. You may already know it by heart, but consider how Jesus explains it:

This, then, is how you should pray:

"Our Father in heaven,
hallowed be your name,
your kingdom come,
your will be done
    on earth as it is in heaven.

Give us today our daily bread.
Forgive us our debts,
    as we also have forgiven our debtors.
And lead us not into temptation,
    but deliver us from the evil one."

For if you forgive men when they sin against you, your heavenly Father will also forgive you. But if you do not forgive men their sins, your Father will not forgive your sins. (Matthew 6:9–15)

As familiar as this passage may be, how often do we really consider what we're praying? Do we *really* want God to answer the part where we pray, "Forgive us our debts, as we also have forgiven our debtors"? Do I really want God to forgive me to the same extent that I forgive others? We all want to receive forgiveness, but when it comes to forgiving the wrongs done to us, it's another story. The aching hurt, the depth of pain, betrayal, disappointment—forgiveness is so difficult to give.

It can be like trying to see clearly in the depths of the sea. To view anything underneath the ocean's surface, you need a mask. And to forgive someone, you have to see beneath the surface as well. On the surface there's no logical reason for me to forgive someone who has hurt me. But when I look below the surface, the Bible gives me some great reasons to forgive.

The first is that Christ commands it. If you've committed your life to knowing and following Him, forgiveness is not an option. Paul wrote plainly to "forgive as the Lord forgave you" (Colossians 3:13). Throughout the Scriptures, forgiveness is not a suggestion. If you want to follow Jesus, it's a commandment. As difficult and emotionally challenging as it may be, we all have to practice forgiveness. We must choose to do it—repeatedly, as necessary. Our feelings and the consequences of the injuries we've suffered may linger, but we're commanded to forgive for a reason: our very survival depends on it.

If you try to dive deep into the ocean without a deep-sea diving suit, you won't survive. The farther down you go into the ocean, the more pressure your body experiences—water, of course, being much denser than air. If you continue to descend, eventually you'll experience so much pressure that your lungs will collapse and your body will be crushed.

Likewise, if you try to live without forgiving, you won't survive. It is essential that we forgive for our own sakes; otherwise we'll drown in bitterness. The deeper you allow yourself to go into the ocean of resentment, the more you'll feel the pressure and the stress. Eventually the pressure will become so intense that your relationships, joy, and health will be crushed. Medical and psychological research reveal that bitterness and resentment have devastating effects. We think that if we hold on to our hurt, we're getting back at the person who injured us. In reality we're just hurting ourselves. If we want to enjoy our lives to the fullest, we must release the bitterness.

Make It Count Moment

How have you experienced the results of bitterness in your life? What were the physical consequences? What's the present impact of bitterness in your life? How is it related to your ability to forgive and be forgiven?

Don't Hold Your Breath

The number one rule in scuba diving is never hold your breath. Instructors drill this into their students because when they're deep underwater and breathe in from the oxygen tank, the air naturally fills their lungs. If they then hold their breath while ascending to the surface, the air in their lungs will expand, stretching and injuring them. It wouldn't be a pleasant experience for your lungs to explode underwater! That's why diving instructors constantly remind their students never to hold their breath.

The number one rule in diving deep into life is never hold in your bitterness. Consider that in most cases we don't develop a festering wound overnight. It usually starts with a little sore that grows into a raging infection. Often the fruits of bitterness are sown with the seeds of anger. "Do not let the sun go down while you are still angry, and do not give the devil a foothold" (Ephesians 4:26–27). Paul wrote that we should never carry our anger for more than a twenty-four-hour period. Why? Because if you take anger into a second day, anger changes: it morphs into bitterness. If you don't breathe out the resentment, you will eventually explode.

We exhale our anger and bitterness by being honest about our feelings, both toward others and toward God. We don't always like to admit that we are hurt, that someone else has managed to offend us. Pride fuels our deception, yet inside we're seething. If our anger goes unchecked, it soon becomes a malignant bitterness.

Often it's not just that we're hurt by others; we're also furious with God. We're thinking, *God, You're the One I'm bitter at because You allowed this. You could've stopped it because You're all powerful, but You let it happen, so You're ultimately responsible.* Then we suppress our feelings because we think we're not supposed to be angry with God. But God is big enough to handle our anger! Besides, He knows we're mad at Him anyway. I used to think that if I admitted I was angry with God, He would probably strike me with a lightning bolt. He doesn't do that. He loves us just the way we are. He wants us to pour out our hearts to Him and admit our feelings and just say, "God, I'm mad. I'm angry. I'm bitter about this. Why did You allow it? I don't understand."

We have to express our feelings to God and arrive at the place where we can pray, "God, I trust that You know what's best. You know I'm mad, so please forgive me and help heal me." When you do that, the healing process begins. That's what happened in David's life. In Psalm 32:5 he said, "Then I acknowledged my sin to you and did not cover up my iniquity. I said, 'I will confess my transgressions to the LORD'—and you forgave the guilt of my sin." When I reveal my heart to God, the healing starts. I breathe out the bitterness, and then I can breathe in forgiveness.

We don't feel like forgiving people who hurt us, but that's okay. Forgiveness is not about what we feel. We forgive because we make a conscious decision and say to God, "I choose to forgive them by Your power because You command me to and because it's for my own good." Then five minutes later, when the hurt comes back to our minds, we can repeat this prayer, as many times as needed. Someone once wisely observed that to forgive is to set a prisoner free and to discover the prisoner was you.

God says you need to forgive for your own sake, because bitterness blocks the blessings He wants to pour into your life. If you open up to God by forgiving and praying for those who hurt you, then blessings can start flowing again. Healing starts to occur in your soul. Jesus was our greatest example of breathing forgiveness.

With one of His last breaths on the cross, He prayed, "Father, forgive them, for they do not know what they are doing" (Luke 23:34). That's where the power to forgive comes from—the realization that we were forgiven first through Christ's sacrifice on the cross.

Drop the Anchor

We can't give what we haven't received. We know we've received forgiveness, but we don't really understand the depth of God's mercy, which makes it that much harder for us to forgive others. If I can understand a little bit of how much Christ has forgiven me, it's a whole lot easier to forgive others who've hurt me.

When we don't confess or embrace the forgiveness so freely given to us, we begin to sink. Think of it—our past mistakes, sins, and failures—as a huge anchor that weighs us down. Some people are so accustomed to dragging an anchor of guilt behind them that they hardly remember it's there. Its effects are devastating nonetheless—anxiety, depression, insomnia, hypertension, and ulcers. Guilt can poison every part of your life.

The good news is that because of God's gift, you don't have to carry around the anchor of guilt that weighs you down. "Once again you will have compassion on us. You will trample our sins under your feet and throw them into the depths of the ocean!" (Micah 7:19, NLT). When you take your anchor of guilt to God, He takes it from you and casts it into the deepest ocean of His forgiveness.

Until you experience the fullness of God's grace and forgiveness, you'll never be able to fully forgive others. You'll never be at peace and see the vision He has for you and your life. You'll never experience the blessings He wants to pour out on you. Forgiveness is not pretending that you weren't really hurt. It's not making light of the offense. Forgiveness is not a shallow experience. Forgiveness means diving deep into honesty and truthfully saying, "What you did hurt me deeply, but I choose to forgive you by God's power."

True forgiveness is about swimming in an ocean that's deeper than we can ever fathom. It's about experiencing a wave of love that washes away our sins, guilt, and bitterness. If you only had one month to live, wouldn't you want to move beyond the shallows into the cleansing ocean of forgiveness?

Make It Last for Life

1. Make a list of the people you need to forgive. Write down the offense—what they did to hurt you—next to each name. Now make a list of all the people from whom you need to ask forgiveness. Next to their names briefly describe how you hurt them. Finally spend time in confession to God. Ask for the power of Christ to wash over you, bathing you in His forgiveness that will enable you to forgive others.

2. Write God a letter and unload on Him. Tell Him all the things you're angry about, all the things you're harboring against Him and wondering about. Be honest, and trust that He can handle anything—everything—you throw at Him, no matter how dark, desperate, or doubtful you may be. Then ask Him to heal your heart as you tear up the letter.

3. Choose a beautiful photograph, seashell, or other memento that represents the ocean. Place it in a prominent place as a reminder to ask God for His forgiveness and to forgive those around you daily.

Everest

SCALING THE OBSTACLES TO UNITY

> We have to pray with our eyes on God,
> not on the difficulties.
> —OSWALD CHAMBERS

> I know God will not give me anything I can't handle.
> I just wish that he didn't trust me so much.
> —MOTHER TERESA

I love to watch those incredible shows about Mount Everest climbers. I'm so intrigued by people who will risk everything to reach the highest place on earth. These guys will fight forty-degrees-below-zero windchill factors, their hands and toes will be frostbitten, they'll barely be able to breathe, but they will give it all to make it to the top. I sit there watching, eating my Twinkie, just exhausted, feeling like I'm right there with them, risking my life.

Mount Everest is over 29,000 feet tall, but when you reach 26,250 feet, you enter what they call the death zone. There the altitude is so high it can't sustain human life. The body is unable to acclimate to such a low level of oxygen, so if you stay in the death zone too long, you die. That's what happened to a climber in May 2006. He was left by climbers in the death zone while they ascended to the top of Everest. All the people who passed him realized he was in trouble, but they assumed he was part of another team and someone else would rescue him.

Not long after that tragedy, another climber, Lincoln Hall, was found in the death zone. He was rescued by a party of four climbers and eleven Sherpas, who gave up their own summit attempt to stay with Hall and descend with him. Hall later fully recovered. What made the difference between the survival of one and the death of the other? Unselfish teamwork.

That kind of teamwork seems to be the exception these days. With sports superstars hogging the glory and corporate leaders taking all the credit, it's rare to see a unified, effective team. Too many individual agendas compete, sabotaging the goal that's best for the team. Whether it's a sports team, a friendship, a business partnership, or a marriage, a lot of relationships fall apart because it's so hard to get along with others. We each have a separate agenda that prevents us from communicating clearly and following through on what's needed to grow closer.

If we were counting the days before we left this earth, we would be looking for ways to build bridges, to bring about healing, and to enjoy our most important relationships. No one wants to leave this earth with unfinished business. We want to leave our loved ones having experienced the summit of our relationships as the result of our courage to love.

Make It Count Moment

How satisfied are you with the state of your most important relationships right now? How would you describe each one—excellent (we've never been closer), okay (we get along, but there's some tension), pretty rough (we're in conflict and floundering), or terrible (we're not going to make it)? What's keeping you from moving toward where you want to be in each one?

Relational Mountain Range

We all know it can be a steep climb from where we are to where we actually want to be. From my experience and the experiences of those I've counseled, it seems there are three mountains that generally prevent unity in relationships.

The first is what I call the mountain of misunderstanding. Most relationships don't have the power to climb over this first summit, and misconceptions and altercations quickly pile up as high as Pikes Peak. In the beginning of a relationship, everything seems so positive. You're climbing a smooth trail together, close beside each other, and then—*wham!*—you're faced with a big boulder of misunderstanding that seems to throw you both off course.

This situation can easily become the death zone for unity in a relationship. In a marriage, it takes just a few months (sometimes only weeks!) to arrive here. That's about the time you emerge from the honeymoon stage and realize you didn't marry a perfect person after all. Or your source of conflict may lie in a business partnership where you seemed to share a corporate vision. After a conflict surfaced, however, you realized that you don't think alike at all. Rather than cling to the ideal—that this spouse, friend, business partner, or team was the right fit and you'd always understand each other—you must realize that differences of opinion are natural and inevitable parts of every relationship. We can't read other people's minds, no matter how much alike we may be. We're all human, so miscommunication and misinterpretations are inevitable.

Another mountain that we must climb in any relationship is what I call the "me first" attitude. It's just human nature to say, "I'll meet your needs but only if you meet my needs first." Whether it's my kids fighting over who gets to ride shotgun in the car or my desire to control the television remote, we all would like to get what we want without thinking about what those around us need. The "me first" attitude leaves others in the death zone while we selfishly pursue the summit.

Obviously, this creates a natural, ongoing conflict. We have to learn how to compromise and discover creative solutions that meet the needs of both people. If we truly love someone, it will be easier to change our agenda—not by becoming a martyr but by having an open dialogue about what's at stake, how both people are feeling, and how things can change.

The third and final peak in this rocky range is the most deadly—the mountain of mistakes. Just as we have misunderstandings and the desire to put ourselves first, we all have faults, and we mess up. Many relationships are forever abandoned on the mountain of mistakes. Every one of us has been hurt by someone else's actions or words. It's easy when you're wounded in a relationship to fortify yourself and refuse to go any farther on this trail because the mountain is just too steep.

You want to protect your heart from being disappointed again. But this only leads you down a different path, back to "me first" mountain, and soon you're so far apart that the relationship is over.

These three mountains shape the landscape of every relationship. We can be intimidated by the ascent, viewing the challenge as insurmountable, and decide to give up. Or we can become the kind of person who knows what it takes to get over the obstacles and keep climbing. None of us truly wants to quit, and if we only had one month to live, this would be clearer than ever. To really love the people in our lives, we have to overcome these relational alps and learn to work through the mistakes and push beyond our self-interests. We have to grow in our willingness and ability to pour ourselves into those we love, motivating them to stay on the trail with us and empowering them to persevere after we're no longer with them.

It's not easy—relationships aren't for wimps. And it's going to take some supernatural help: God's power to love. But the supply is limitless, and the price of His resources never goes up, because they're free.

Make It Count Moment

Which of these three mountains—misunderstandings, "me first," or mistakes—has derailed your key relationships most recently? How did you handle the situation? What would you do differently if you could?

The Rope of Acceptance

The Bible reveals strategies for keeping relational mountains small and manageable. In order to persevere and improve our relationships, we first must connect with the rope of acceptance. Rock climbers use a technique with ropes called belaying. It involves securing a climber to a rope so he doesn't fall too far if he slips off the rock. Similarly, we can't climb to new heights safely if we don't connect with a rope of acceptance. "Accept one another, then, just as Christ accepted you, in order to bring praise to God" (Romans 15:7). One of our greatest problems in relationships is that we're always trying to change the people we're relating to. To accept others means that we stop trying to *change* them and we start trying to *understand* them.

Easier said than done, right? Absolutely. But in over twenty years of marriage, I've learned a valuable secret: *acceptance means to stop trying to change my spouse and to start cherishing them.* I really haven't accepted someone if I'm still focused on changing them. Cherishing people simply means to value them enough to seek to understand them. To be honest, it's not natural for me to totally accept the people in my life. My selfish inclination is to try to change the people I interact with and attempt to make them more like me. It's supernatural to accept the people in my life just the way they are, work on my own faults and character flaws, and trust God to deal with other people. As He gives us the power to accept one another, we learn to really connect with the rope of acceptance and climb to greater heights together.

Traction with Action

In conjunction with acceptance, we gain traction with loving action. Nothing is more important to climbers than the traction of their boots. You can have all the other equipment, but if you aren't surefooted, you'll never ascend difficult terrain. The essentials for strong relationships are those small loving actions, all the seemingly insignificant things that mean so much to someone else. When you are inconsistent, telling others how important they are but never following through with loving actions, then the relationships will falter. The clarity and security your loving actions bring to the people around you can't be underestimated and will provide the traction to take you to the summit.

Every climber also knows the importance of being tethered to the rock in order to keep from falling. It's a fail-safe attachment point for protection. In our relationships that tether is forgiveness. It's the loving action that can keep a relationship growing and maturing over time. The best relationships are built on forgiveness, because all relationships involve imperfect people who make mistakes. Six powerful words keep you connected as you scale the mountain of mistakes: I'm sorry. Will you forgive me?

Obstacles—misunderstanding, selfishness, mistakes—are part of every relationship, but we can overcome them and grow closer to the ones we love if we're willing to practice acceptance, loving actions, and ongoing forgiveness. This kind of behavior requires God's supernatural love infusing us, helping us push beyond our natural inclinations and expectations. He's more than willing and always available to help us love others as He loves us. With the proper gear that God provides, we can not only share the view from the summit but enjoy the climb as well.

Make It Last for Life

1. Diagnose and write down what you think each important relationship in your life needs in order to be healthier. It may be as simple as spending more time together, discussing a glaring but as yet unspoken issue, or sending someone a note or e-mail to say you're thinking about them.

2. How do you communicate your commitment to those you love? Do you tend to tell more than you show or show more than you tell? Psychologists say that most of us tend to favor one method over the other—we say how we feel but may not show it as much, or we show it consistently and assume our actions speak for us. Determine which style you favor, and practice the other today with those you love most.

3. Spend time in prayer today for each person you consider essential to your life. Ask God to reveal how you can improve your relationships with these vitally important people.

Boxing Ring

RESOLVING CONFLICTS BY FIGHTING FAIR

> The opposite of love is not hate,
> it's indifference.
> —ELIE WIESEL

> They may forget what you said,
> but they will never forget how you made them feel.
> —CARL W. BUECHNER

Growing up with Muhammad Ali and the *Rocky* movies, I've always admired boxers—their strength, agility, resilience, and determination. Something about the way they approach a fight fascinates me so much that I recently visited Lee Canalito's Boxing Gym in downtown Houston, where I worked with Ray Sugaroso to learn how to box. His goal was to train me to go a few rounds with some of the gym's best fighters. My goal was to avoid permanent damage to my middle-aged body!

I survived but gained a whole new respect for boxers. Even though my opponents took it easy on me, one landed a blow to my chin that gave me a headache for the rest of the week. I learned that while I'm a fair fighter, I'm probably not going to Las Vegas to compete for a world title anytime soon. Truth be told, I didn't really have a clue about boxing before Ray and his crew got me into the ring.

Just as I had no idea how to box, most of us have no idea how to resolve conflict. Conflict is inevitable in relationships; when two unique and imperfect people come together, they simply won't agree about everything. That's why it's critical that we learn how to deal effectively with relationship issues. No one really teaches us how to confront and resolve the impasses that life inevitably brings, especially in marriage. I think there ought to be a law that before you get married, you have to take a class on resolving conflict. But even in friendships, teams at work, committees, and extended family, it's tough to know when to hold your ground and when to throw in the towel. If you only had one month to live, you would want to know how to push through those lingering issues and finally resolve conflicts with the ones you love.

Fighting Fair

The Bible provides us with principles for a fair fight. While I want to concentrate on how they apply to your relationship with your spouse, they also apply to business partners, co-workers, and friends. These principles don't guarantee you'll win or be right every time a disagreement flares up, but they do ensure you'll grow closer to those you love through the process of confronting conflict.

One guideline that sounds simple can be the most difficult to maintain: stay in the ring and off the ropes. Sometimes the conflict gets a little heated and messy, but in our primary relationships we have to have enough courage to stay in the ring until we come to a resolution, no matter how long that takes. If we really love someone, then we must summon the stamina to confront and push through the unpleasant emotions that come with conflict. Those feelings can be so powerful and nasty that we work hard to avoid them. Men typically withdraw when faced with strong emotions because they feel uncomfortable dealing with them. Consequently, some men get out of the combat zone when problems begin to surface because they're committed to avoiding an argument at all costs. Few things are more frustrating to a woman than when her husband dodges a conflict and goes into his cave where he becomes distant, detached, and aloof.

We've all devised conflict-management tactics that reflect our temperaments, our experiences, or the examples we had growing up. Most of us have embraced one of five primary styles of fighting. The first is what I call the rope-a-dope fighter, a style invented by Muhammad Ali in his prime. In the heat of the fight, he would lean into and bounce against the ropes, covering himself up and no longer swinging a punch. His opponent would think, *He's tired—I've got him now,* and would come over to the ropes and start punching away at him. But the other boxer wouldn't really hurt him. Ali would bounce around on the ropes, conserving all his energy while his opponent got frustrated and flailed away at him. Ultimately, the opponent would wear himself out.

Rope-a-dope fighters are "no way" resolvers, people who say, "There's no way you're getting me into a fight." They avoid conflict, refuse to engage, and retreat when emotions arise. Their number one rule is avoid conflict at all costs. You see the problem, though. Avoiding conflict at all costs may produce a fragile peace, but it undermines the relationship, keeping it shallow and fear based. Without resolution, the relationship stays at a surface level and never develops the intimacy that comes from working through tough issues.

Next is the knockout artist, the one whose fighting stance is "It's my way or the highway." These relational boxers fight until they win and the other person gives in. The knockout artist says, "I'm always right, and I want my way every time." While knockout artists usually win, the relationships go down for the count because the other person has no voice and will eventually quit trying.

Then there's the take-the-fall fighter. These fighters throw in the towel early. They're always the first to give in. They become doormats, martyrs, as they roll over and play dead. This produces a false peace and ultimately creates tremendous bitterness in the person who always gives in and dangerous pride in the one who doesn't. It's not a healthy way to fight.

Fourth, the one-two puncher is committed to a give-and-take resolution. You win half, and I'll win half. I give in sometimes; you give in sometimes. This style can be healthier and more effective than the others because there's at least a willingness to stay in the ring and an expectation that either can win.

However, the best style is the sparring partner, the person committed to being a teammate and helping their partner. Sparring partners stay in the ring and off the ropes. Regardless of how unpleasant it becomes, they stay at it until they come to a mutual decision that they feel is best for both. Sparring partners realize the relationship is more important than anything they could argue about, and they understand that the process is usually more vital than the outcome.

If time were running out and you were counting the remaining days, wouldn't you want to achieve real peace with those you love? The only way is to stay in the ring, settling any unresolved conflicts before it's too late. From my experience with those who know their time is limited, it's one of the greatest gifts they can give to those they love.

Make It Count Moment

Which style of fighter are you? How do you think this style developed? How would you describe the way your parents handled conflict? How did their style influence yours? If you had one month to live, what would you change about the way you handle conflict? Why?

Ground Rules

If we're going to stay in the ring in order for the relationship to grow, then we must commit to a fair fight. In boxing, the referee brings the two boxers to the center of the ring and says, "Okay, we're going to have a fair fight. Here are the ground rules—no punching below the belt, no gouging, no tripping, and"—in case Mike Tyson's involved—"no biting." The rules are laid out, and they shape the expectations and actions of both contenders.

Before you fight with your mate or someone you care about, you must establish the ground rules, some limits that will not be exceeded. Before you have a confrontation with a co-worker, you have to remind the other person that you're committed to finding a solution together, not creating a scapegoat. Before you sit down to resolve an issue with a dear friend, you need to restate your commitment to them and to the friendship. The friend needs to know you're willing to endure the unpleasant feelings that come with confrontation because you value the relationship and want to preserve it.

At the start of a match, boxers put in mouth guards for protection. We must put in a mouth guard as well. Paul gives us the ultimate mouth guard in his letter to the Ephesians: "Do not use harmful words,…only helpful words, the kind that build up and provide what is needed" (4:29, GNT). Words can cut deeply, and the wound can linger and fester for years. We must be willing to take control of our language, especially in the heat of the fight, if we hope to build the relationship beyond the present conflict. It has been said that the real art of conversation is not only saying the right thing at the right time but also learning to leave unsaid the wrong thing at the tempting moment. This doesn't mean we avoid talking about the heart of the conflict. We don't ignore it or neglect it, but we honestly reveal our true feelings, even though sparks may fly. Agree at the start that some words are off-limits. Don't throw out the *d* word, *divorce,* as a live grenade in the middle of an argument with your spouse. Express the intensity of your feelings without profane or abusive language. These words only clog the real communication that will get you through the conflict.

After your mouth guard is in, the next ground rule for a fair fight is don't attack. Learn to attack the issues without attacking each other. Never say, "You did this. It's all your fault. You're such a liar." When you attempt to blame and name, the other person's walls go up, and you won't get anywhere. You'll never move to reconciliation when you're both on the offensive. Launching missiles over those walls will just drive you farther apart rather than bring you closer together.

Instead of attacking, try to own your feelings. If both of you will accept responsibility for your mistakes, then you'll be sparring and growing together rather than wounding and regretting. So start with your feelings. No one can discount your feelings; they're valid simply by being yours. The key is expressing them without letting them consume the conflict.

Another strategy is to avoid dragging history into the current conflict. It can be so tempting to unroll the laundry list of offenses, grievances, and disappointments that you've documented throughout your relationship with the other person. This only diverts attention from the conflict at hand. Decide to focus on the immediate issue and stay at it until you reach resolution. When you get historical, don't be surprised if the other person gets hysterical.

These are ground rules, some guidelines to lay out ahead of time. Commit to fighting fair, and you'll be surprised at how you can reach resolution more quickly and make the relationship stronger. Stay in the ring, face the fight in front of you, and focus on fighting fair.

Make It Count Moment

Do you usually fight fair with your loved ones? Which of these ground rules is hardest for you to keep? Or in other words, how do you usually hit below the belt? How have others responded to this tactic?

Split Decisions

In marriage it's crucial to stay in the ring, fight fair, and come out with an "our way" solution that you both feel good about and that strengthens the relationship. But every once in a while, you may face an occasion when you can't agree. In these situations focus on reconciliation rather than resolution. Remember that your relationship is more important than agreeing on every single thing. So disagree agreeably.

You can walk hand in hand without seeing eye to eye on every single thing. "Wisdom…is peace-loving and courteous. It allows discussion and is willing to yield to others" (James 3:17, TLB). Mature relationships can handle the rare fights when it's a split decision. You'll discover there are some things you'll never agree on. I don't care how much you both love the Lord and how totally in love you are with each other, you'll never agree on everything, because God made you different. It's not a matter of right and wrong. It's a matter of seeing life from different perspectives.

If you're committed to keeping an open mind, to accepting the other person's point of view, then you can maintain respect for each other even when you agree to disagree. This is not compromise, at least not the negative, quick-fix kind that agrees to disagree just to keep the peace and move on. Split decisions allow for, and even appreciate, the unique perspective you each bring to the conflict.

The most important thing you can do is to bring the Prince of Peace into the ring with you. It takes three to build a great marriage: a husband, a wife, and God. You don't just bring Him into your corner and say, "God, help me win this argument." No, you invite Him into the whole situation because He's the only one who can meet your deepest needs. Bringing Him into the fight doesn't mean you become passive and pliable. Jesus got angry and expressed His emotions. But as the perfect Son of God, He never sinned, so that shows me that anger is okay. It's not necessarily a sin; in fact, sometimes anger is the most appropriate emotion you can have when you care deeply about a relationship. But we must be willing to deal with our anger and channel it the way Jesus did: toward achieving His Father's will, toward loving others. The key is to learn to walk with Him daily. This is the real secret to reconciling, to overcoming conflict, to fighting fair: become more like Jesus.

Make It Last for Life

1. Describe in writing the last major conflict you faced with a loved one. Imagine that you're a spectator, even a commentator, and analyze the fight. Was it a fair fight? Were ground rules maintained? How would you describe the fighting styles of the contenders? Who won the match? Was it a clean win?

2. Which of your present relationships involve conflicts that would require you to step into the ring if you knew you only had one month to live?

3. Spend time in prayer, asking God to show you when and how you look to other people to meet needs that only He can meet. Ask Him to provide what you need most from Him.

Sandpaper

SMOOTHING THE EDGES

> Remember that everyone you meet is afraid of something,
> loves something and has lost something.
> —H. JACKSON BROWN JR.

> The only people with whom you should try to get even
> are those who have helped you.
> —JOHN E. SOUTHARD

M aybe you read the prior chapter and thought, *Yeah, this is all good stuff about how to resolve conflicts, but you don't know how many people I have to deal with who just really irritate me, even some of my family. I love them, but they drive me crazy.* No matter how hard we try to be accepting, most of us will always have people in our lives who are difficult to love and get along with. It's just human nature. But if we were down to our last month, we would want to see beyond the surface issues that irritate us. In order to improve these relationships, we must reframe the way we see them.

We all know that sanding can be very useful when it comes to woodworking or finishing furniture. But if you take sandpaper and rub it against your skin, it doesn't feel good. It's abrasive and painful. There are certain people in our lives who are just as hurtful and annoying. They irritate us. They rub us the wrong way. They get under our skin.

You may encounter sandpaper people every single day at your workplace. Some of them may even live in your house with you! Often it's the people we love the most who irritate us the most. But how often do you stop to think about how you bother those around you? You may be the sandpaper person in the midst of your family and friends. The reality is that we're *all* sandpaper people. We all irritate other people at times, and that's part of God's plan for our lives.

Yes, you read correctly. Sandpaper people are part of God's plan for your life. He allows sandpaper people into your life so He can craft you into a sharper tool for His purposes. Paul explains, "For we are God's workmanship, created in Christ Jesus to do good works, which God prepared in advance for us to do" (Ephesians 2:10). In the Greek the word for "workmanship" literally means "a work of art or a masterpiece." God is crafting you into the perfect tool to accomplish His amazing plan for you.

This puts a fantastic twist on those relationships that annoy us. They are allowed into our lives for our own good, to smooth away our rough edges and make us more like Christ. This sounds wonderfully spiritual, but the problem is, how do we get along with all the other tools in the shed? Some folks seem to rub us the wrong way no matter how we try to work together. If only they were more like us, then we'd all enjoy complete harmony, right? Other than being completely unrealistic, such bliss would also rob us of becoming all that God wants us to be.

Make It Count Moment

Who are the sandpaper people in your life presently—maybe someone in your family, maybe a co-worker, a boss, an employee, a friend, or a neighbor? How often do you have to interact with them? How do you usually relate to them?

Toolshed Trials

The Bible provides us with a guiding principle for getting along with sandpaper people and having a lasting impact in our relationships. It's not easy, but implementing this principle can dramatically change our relational dynamics. If we are not only to tolerate but to grow in our sandpaper relationships, then we need to gain the Carpenter's perspective on people and performance. We have to learn to see the difficult people in our lives in a new light.

The first step in this process is to identify how other people bug you. While every individual is unique and every relationship special, I've found some categories helpful in thinking about our relational irritants. The first group reminds me of a measuring tape: these people always let you know that you don't quite measure up. As insatiable perfectionists, they feel compelled to set the standards for everyone else. They continue measuring again and again, knowing that others will never be exactly on the mark. In short, they judge by their own standards of righteousness.

Another type of person you may recognize is the hammer. Hammers tend to be as subtle as a freight train, pushing their agendas on others and forcing their way. Everyone walks on eggshells around a hammer, because you never know when the hammer's going to come down! They can be loud and demanding or subtle and manipulative, but they're stubbornly committed to using the force of their own will to get their way.

Next we come to those people who seem naturally gifted at cutting others down. In an argument, skill saws know just the thing to say that will hurt the most. The words may be sarcastic or straightforward, but these people have an uncanny ability to cut to the quick and leave others bleeding on the floor. Skill saws win verbal arguments every time—not because they're right, but because they know where to cut to weaken the other's platform.

Do you have any vise grips in your life? You know, people who get a grip on you and don't know when to let go? They are extra needy and usually squeeze the life out of those around them. These folks have no clue when it comes to social and relational boundaries. They bounce from one crisis to the next, needing constant support and encouragement. A vise grip clamps down on your life, affecting all your other relationships.

In life's toolbox we also run across grinders, people with explosive personalities just waiting to go off and send the sparks flying. Related to the grinders are the axes, those who constantly cut a wide swath in their wake. They tend to be negative, always grumbling and looking for ways to tear down the hopes and plans of others. Their cousins, the hatchets, usually take smaller chops but hold on to past hurts and grudges much longer. They don't know how to—you guessed it—bury the hatchet.

Last but not least are the putty people. These are the people in your life who have no consistency, no backbone. Eager to please and always agreeable, they change like chameleons so that you never know who they really are or what they really think. Putty people always say yes even when they're already spread too thin.

When we catalog them like this, it's tempting to think, *How in the world am I supposed to get along with so many irritating tools in the shed?* Or you may be thinking I just described everyone in your family to a *T*! In either case, we must learn to see beyond the damage each of these tools can render and instead determine how we can construct a meaningful future together.

Make It Count Moment

Think back to the sandpaper people you listed earlier in this chapter. How does each fit into one of these categories of tools? Which tools bother you the most? Why?

The Carpenter's Perspective

Nobody I know is normal. You're not normal. I'm not normal. We're all unique. There is no one else in the world like you. Even though we're vastly different, we're all in the same toolbox. And instead of working together to build lasting relationships, as God intends, we're often tempted to criticize. It's always much easier for us to point out someone else's faults and flaws rather than look at our own.

Jesus talks about this in Matthew 7: "Why do you look at the speck of sawdust in your brother's eye and pay no attention to the plank in your own eye? How can you say to your brother, 'Let me take the speck out of your eye,' when all the time there is a plank in your own eye? You hypocrite, first take the plank out of your own eye, and then you will see clearly to remove the speck from your brother's eye" (verses 3–5).

We have sharp vision when it comes to finding the sawdust in everybody else's eyes. We see this little speck of sawdust, this fault, problem, sin, or character flaw in someone else's life, and we can't wait to point it out. We exclaim, "You've really got a problem there!" "But," Jesus says, "here's the real issue. You're trying to get the sawdust out of someone's eye when you've got a two-by-four in your own eye." There is a whole lumberyard of two-by-four people walking around saying, "Man, did you see that problem in their lives? My goodness, I'm glad I'm not like them." They're so fixated on pointing out everyone else's splinters that they totally miss the planks sticking out of their own lives.

Notice that Jesus doesn't say to ignore the sawdust. Many people today think that whenever you point something out as sin, you're being judgmental. This isn't the case at all. We're to look at the sawdust in people's eyes and help heal them with Christ's power. Our role is not to judge but to be healing agents. However, sometimes we come up to them and say, "Hey, you know you've got some sawdust in your eye. Let me help you with that," and then we hit them over the head with the telephone pole sticking out of our own eye. They end up thinking, *Thanks, but no thanks. I'd rather have the sawdust in my eye than get hit upside the head with that thing.*

In our families we can be so quick to point out the faults in everybody else and overlook the glaring weaknesses in ourselves. I've discovered that if I concentrate on my own shortcomings and let God give me the courage to face my own faults, character flaws, and mistakes, then I don't feel the urgency to help others see their specks. If I forget about trying to change everybody else and simply work on letting God change me, then the people in my life are much more open to me.

The Strength of Sawdust

When you put sawdust under intense heat and pressure, it becomes a solid building material known as particle board. Most of us have seen it around our homes without realizing what it's made from. It's heavy, strong, and frequently used in construction.

Similarly, God allows some sandpaper people and toolshed trials into our lives for one reason: to increase the heat and pressure so we will become stronger. He's much more interested in our character than in our comfort. Paul describes the "particle process" this way: "We can rejoice, too, when we run into problems and trials for we know that they are good for us—they help us learn to be patient. And patience develops strength of character in us and helps us trust God more each time we use it until finally our hope and faith are strong and steady" (Romans 5:3–4, TLB).

As uncomfortable or unsettling as we may find it, God intentionally places some people in our lives to rub us the wrong way, to smooth the rough edges of our character, so that we're more like Jesus. It's part of His plan to make my character strong and steady, so God allows people and pressure to build my character. Even our critics can teach us and help us grow. We should be selective and not absorb all the criticism that comes our way, nor should we categorically dismiss it. Instead I favor the chewing-gum approach to criticism: chew it and spit it out— don't swallow it. Take advantage of criticism by chewing on it, absorbing the 10 percent or so that's valid, learning from it, and then spitting out the other 90 percent. Don't swallow it whole, but allow the flavor of criticism to help you grow.

God wants you to learn from the sandpaper people in your life. He has placed them in your life for a reason. Some of you have a hammer in your life. Did you ever stop to think that maybe God has allowed that hammer so you will learn to be strong and stand up to him or her instead of being weak and walked on like a doormat? Maybe God is trying to build you into a stronger leader by giving you the opportunity to stand up to that hammer even though it's uncomfortable.

You may have a measuring tape in your life. Did you ever consider that God has allowed that measuring tape so you will learn to look to Him for approval rather than to this person? God reminds us to stay humble and rely on Him when we find ourselves bristling with anger, fear, or irritation. To view relationships with a new perspective, we need to recognize the positive benefit God intends them to have in our lives. The next time someone sets you off, pause for a moment and ask God a few questions: *What are You trying to teach me? What are You trying to build in my character? What are You trying to show me about leadership? What are You trying to reveal to me about life?*

Finally, you get a whole new perspective on the difficult people in your life when you realize that not only has God placed them in your life for a reason but He has placed *you* in their lives for a reason. He wants you to reveal some of His love, His patience, His mercy toward them. You may be the only face of Jesus they'll ever see. God wants you to surprise them with His love in ways that only you can.

Make It Last for Life

1. Read the descriptions of the various tool types again. Which tool best describes the way you sometimes come across to those around you? Are you more of a hammer, a skill saw, an ax, or something else? The truth is that most of us are multipurpose tools and react differently depending on the context and our chemistry with others. Consider how your different relationships bring out different defensive or offensive reactions.

2. How often are you tempted to point out the problems in someone else's life—rarely, occasionally, frequently? What usually motivates your observations concerning the specks of others? Spend time in prayer asking God to help you remove the two-by-fours in your own life before speaking about someone else's specks.

3. Describe one person in your life who consistently rubs you the wrong way. How have you attempted to relate to him or her in the past? If you knew you only had one month to live, what would you want to tell this person? What's keeping you from speaking up today?

The Gift

THANKING THOSE AROUND YOU

Gratitude unlocks the fullness of life.
It turns what we have into enough, and more.
It turns denial into acceptance,
chaos to order, confusion to clarity.
It can turn a meal into a feast,
a house into a home, a stranger into a friend.
—MELODY BEATTIE

We can only be said to be alive in those moments
when our hearts are conscious of our treasures.
—THORNTON WILDER

*T*he taste of warm apple pie. The smell of wood smoke on a crisp fall evening. The sound of small children squealing with delight on Christmas morning. The way the sun looks setting over the mountains. The feel of sand between your toes at the beach. Special time spent around a delicious meal with family and close friends.

Most people who know their days are numbered understand the importance of the little sensory details that we often take for granted. They know what it means to wake up each day with a grateful heart. I've seen men and women suffering chronic pain with smiles on their faces as they sipped their morning coffee or held the hand of their spouse. They were immeasurably grateful for one more day, for another opportunity to embrace their lives in every detail.

We talk about gratitude a lot in our culture but find it difficult to practice. The consumer mind-set instilled by media and advertising, combined with our human tendency to compare, leaves us coming up short. We're told—and often believe—that what we have isn't enough. We're conditioned to automatically accept that the next electronic gadget, the next pair of designer shoes, the next tropical vacation, or the next romantic relationship will fulfill us. But of course material goods, exciting experiences, and even other people can't quench the spiritual thirst in our lives.

Only God can slake our deepest thirst with His living water. As we've explored in prior chapters, when we look to Him first, we become free to give much more of ourselves to those around us. Cicero wisely observed, "Gratitude is not only the greatest of virtues, but the parent of all the others." When we are thankful, we become content and full of the peace that only He can provide. Focusing on how grateful we are for what we have prevents us from becoming bitter and greedy for more.

Make It Count Moment

When was the last time you remember stopping to savor a rich moment? What were the circumstances—were you on vacation, with family, at Thanksgiving? What prevents you from noticing more of these moments?

Second Chances

Jesus' experience as recorded in Luke 17 is an example of how even people who are given a second chance at life sometimes forget to thank the source of all good things. "Now on his way to Jerusalem, Jesus traveled along the border between Samaria and Galilee. As he was going into a village, ten men who had leprosy met him. They stood at a distance and called out in a loud voice, 'Jesus, Master, have pity on us!'" (verses 11–13). These ten men had one thing in common—their plight was hopeless.

Leprosy was the most dreaded disease of Jesus' day. It always began with blotches on the skin, which then turned into lumps, which eventually would grow so large that the person would be disfigured beyond recognition. Then in the next stage, fingers and toes would literally fall off. Ultimately the person's life would end in coma and death. It was an excruciating, terrifying way to die.

In Jesus' day the first sign of leprosy was a death sentence. Once identified, the leper was forced to leave home, family, and friends and was cast outside the city. A strict law even stated that people with leprosy couldn't get within fifty yards of a person who didn't have the disease. If they did, they were pelted with rocks and stoned to death.

Can you imagine never being touched again, never feeling the hug of a child, never feeling the arm of a parent around your shoulders, never feeling the embrace of your spouse? That's what these ten men had experienced for years. Some of them had probably had leprosy since they were children, because the disease took so long to progress. They'd given up hope after they had tried everything and nothing had worked. But then something amazing happened. They encountered the Carpenter from Nazareth, the One said to be the Messiah. "He [Jesus] looked at them and said, 'Go show yourselves to the priests.' And as they went, their leprosy disappeared" (Luke 17:14, NLT).

It was incredibly rare for someone to be healed of leprosy, but apparently it had happened before, because a law existed requiring a leper who was healed to go to the priest. The priest would determine whether or not the leper was cleansed and would be allowed to return to his family, friends, and community. So it's striking that Jesus told these ten lepers to go to the priest *before* they were healed, as if their health had already been restored. It was a test of their faith. Did they really believe Jesus was who He said He was? They obeyed and passed the test.

Just imagine this ragged bunch of men as they were walking to the temple. They looked down and saw the blotches on their skin had completely disappeared, and they quickly realized they were healed. They could go home again! Such an unbelievable gift was surely celebrated—jumping and shouting and whatever their equivalent to high-fiving might've been. So much incredulous joy and such urgency to get to the priest, to get home, to get their lives back. But along the way, one of them stopped and said, "Hey, wait a minute, guys. I have to go back and thank the One responsible for this. I have to express my gratitude to the Giver of this incredible gift." The other ones might have said, "What do you mean? We have to go to our families. We haven't seen them in years." But he must have responded, "Yes, but first I want to go back and thank Jesus."

Three Sizes

Perhaps the most significant part of this entire story occurred next. "One of them, when he saw he was healed, came back, praising God in a loud voice. He threw himself at Jesus' feet and thanked him—and he was a Samaritan. Jesus asked, 'Were not all ten cleansed? Where are the other nine? Was no one found to return and give praise to God except this foreigner?'" (Luke 17:15–18). This guy was from another country, yet he was the only one who came back to thank Jesus. "Then he [Jesus] said to him, 'Rise and go; your faith has made you well'" (verse 19). This man finally had what you and I take for granted each and every day. He had new life. He had his health. He would live to see tomorrow. But he realized it was a precious gift that God had given him, so he went back to thank Jesus. The hard truth about the whole story is that he was the *only one.* Out of ten, he was the only one who expressed gratitude. He went back and threw himself at Christ's feet.

Gratitude has the power to change us completely. This former leper was not just physically healed; he was also spiritually healed. There is power in gratitude to heal us spiritually, emotionally, and relationally. An attitude of gratitude opens up our hearts to God, enabling us to really see the world the way it is, to experience life to its fullest and enjoy each breath. That's the power of thankfulness, but you can almost hear the hurt in Jesus' heart as He asked three questions: Weren't there ten? Where are the other nine? Did only one come back to thank Me?

Now before we judge too harshly the nine who didn't come back to thank Jesus, we need to look at our own lives. What is it about our human hearts that allows us to take so many things for granted? The very thing we desperately want, once we get it, we don't thank God for. How often do we get in a jam and plead with God to provide what we need? "God, I'll do anything," we say. "Just help me this one time, and I'm yours for the rest of my life." When He does provide, even if it's not always exactly what we want when we want it, we neglect to thank Him.

On that day ten men received a gift, but only one unwrapped it. Ten people received life that day, but only one realized there was more to his life than his time on earth. This is what gratitude does—it changes you. It opens your heart to God so you can experience all the blessings He has for you.

When I think about the way gratitude can increase our capacity to love, I think of Dr. Seuss's *How the Grinch Stole Christmas!* My favorite line in the whole story occurs right after the Grinch has realized the true meaning of Christmas: "And some say the Grinch's heart grew three sizes that day." Gratitude expands our hearts the same way. We become fully aware of the details of the life we love, the simple things that delight us, and, perhaps most of all, the people God has placed in our lives. Simply stated, gratitude expands our capacity to enjoy life.

Make It Count Moment

On most days are you more like the one who returned to thank Jesus or the nine who went their own way? How often do you thank those around you for what they contribute to your life? Who would you want to thank today if you only had one month to live?

One in Ten

Ingratitude has the opposite effect. It causes our hearts to shrink and become colder. It blocks the flow of God's wisdom and blessings in our lives. In fact, the opposite of a heart of gratitude is a heart of dissatisfaction, grumbling, complaints, and negativity. Whenever I'm being negative, I can't help but feel that God is disappointed with my attitude, that it's a slap in His face after all He's given me.

When I think about the odds—one in ten—that Jesus experienced with the lepers, I realize the percentages are pretty much the same today. Maybe 10 percent of the people in the world today are fully alive. They truly appreciate the gifts God has given them, and their eyes are wide open to the sacred gift of life. They celebrate each new day and are deeply grateful to God for it. They take advantage of every breath, every moment, and every opportunity to celebrate life.

But I would guess that about 90 percent of the people in the world today never stop to thank God for the blessings in their lives, never savor the richness of the gift of life. Never. Sometimes I'm in the 10 percent, with my eyes wide open as I fully appreciate every moment, living life to the fullest out of a heart of gratitude. But many times I'm in the 90 percent, busy going from thing to thing, event to event, rushing around doing countless activities that seem urgent. I become myopic, my eyes narrowly focused on my little world, and I miss out on the big picture of life.

If you only had one month to live, you'd want to make the most of it. To laugh and fully engage with the people you love. To appreciate the little things, the ones that might seem silly to others but that delight your soul, and to give God thanks for allowing you to experience them. Whether it's the smell of buttered popcorn at the theater or the view from a beautiful mountaintop, the taste of our mothers' fried chicken or the way a child's hand feels clinging to ours, we are all blessed with rich moments. When we thank those around us, it only increases the love between us. When we express our gratitude to God, it increases our capacity to experience a full life without regrets.

Make It Last for Life

1. Make a gratitude list of five or six little things that you often take for granted. Stop and smell the roses by thanking God for the small things that make life beautiful.

2. Look back over your list and choose one item to experience today. It might mean savoring your favorite meal. It might be listening to a favorite CD you haven't heard in a while. It could be smelling a fresh pot of coffee brewing. Whatever you choose, try to relish it.

3. Make a list of the people in your life for whom you're most grateful. Try to think beyond the obvious ones—family and friends—and consider the people who contribute to your life each day yet tend to be overlooked. Whether it's your child's teacher, your assistant at the office, the bus driver on your commute, or the barista at the coffee shop, make a point to thank them today.

Last Call

REVEALING YOUR HEART

Say what you want to say
when you have the feeling and the chance.
My deepest regrets are the things I did not do,
the opportunities missed and the things unsaid.
—JIM KELLER

He became what we are
that He might make us what He is.
—SAINT ATHANASIUS

*I*n 1876 when Alexander Graham Bell spoke the first words into a crude invention called the telephone, no one could have imagined how the world would soon shrink as the lines of communication expanded to connect us all. But like every great invention that creates convenience, it also created complications.

Today we have satellite, teleconference, wireless, mobile, and hands-free communication abilities. While it seems you can reach anybody, anywhere, anytime, I wonder how often real connection occurs. Lines of communication are breaking down with alarming frequency—between husbands and wives, parents and teenagers, bosses and employees, co-workers, and friends. People talk all the time but rarely seem to hear each other's words, let alone their unspoken messages.

Experts tell us that 80 percent of all communication is nonverbal: facial expressions, hand gestures, body language. So when we talk to someone on the phone, we're only expressing about 20 percent of what we're trying to convey. Now I'm not advocating throwing away your cell phone. But if you only had one month to live, it would be time to get serious about communicating with those around you.

In order to express your love to the key people in your life, it's essential that you tell them what you consider most important, ask their forgiveness, and remind them of shared times. You need to listen, perhaps for the first time, to what your loved ones are really saying to you. You must repair misunderstandings and broken lines of communication. If we're going to live as though we only have four weeks left, we have to be willing to move from communication breakdown to communication breakthrough. Billions of words are spoken every day in our homes, offices, churches, and schools, but in order to really connect, we must start with the most powerful Word of all.

Make It Count Moment

Right now in your life do you have a relationship in which the lines of communication are really breaking down? Was there a lack of communication, a miscommunication, or a discrepancy between words and actions? How have you responded to this person?

Lost in Translation

If you've ever studied a foreign language, you know how much of the intended meaning can be altered or even lost in the translation process. Even when we're using the same language, that can be true. That's why it's vitally important to give words a context. The people around us need to know what is ultimately motivating our communication with them. The only way they can truly know our intention is if we pay the price of revealing our heart. Like the old-fashioned pay phones, we must make a deposit into the relationship before there's a dial tone. Before you open your mouth to speak, you must first open your heart. As Oswald

Chambers put it, "It is the unseen and the spiritual in people that determines the outward and the actual."

The most dramatic example of an open heart speaking is one that changed the course of history and continues to redirect countless lives today: "The Word became flesh and made his dwelling among us. We have seen his glory, the glory of the One and Only, who came from the Father, full of grace and truth" (John 1:14). Jesus communicated with us by leaving His home in heaven, coming to this earth, and putting on human flesh so He could reveal His heart to us. He opened up His heart and made Himself totally vulnerable. He risked rejection and was, in fact, misunderstood by many, especially those in power.

Why did He do it? For one reason—so we could see what God is like. So He could communicate with us in the most effective way possible—as the Word that transcends all language barriers. Until we open up our hearts to those we love, we will never experience a communication breakthrough. Before the words flow, our hearts must be exposed. We have to risk vulnerability to the point of possible rejection.

One vital way we open our hearts to those around us is by sharing our time. In our overloaded lives we often try to relate to others efficiently, doing what saves us time, energy, and money. But whenever we skimp on communication in a relationship in order to be efficient, all effectiveness is lost. Relationships don't exist and grow according to rules of efficiency. It costs time to communicate effectively, but keep in mind that we pay the price in relationships when we neglect them. Dates with our spouses. Activities and outings with our kids. Meals and celebrations with our friends. Team-building time with co-workers. Often these are the first things we drop when we get busy and need more time at the office. But if we were counting down our days, we would most likely wish we had invested more of our time this way.

Not only must we share our time, but we also need to share our troubles. For people to see my heart, I have to admit my needs. Too often we're like the character in a children's book titled *The Knight in Rusty Armor*. The fearless knight rides off to slay dragons and fight fierce battles, but when he comes home, he doesn't know how to take off his armor. We have to learn how to take off our armor so we can connect with others. Sure we have to wear armor; otherwise we can't fight the battles we inevitably need to fight. Both social and professional boundaries are necessary. But if you want to have a breakthrough in any relationship, whether it's with a co-worker, an employee, your boss, your husband, your wife, or your teenager, you have to learn when to take off the armor and be vulnerable and expose your heart and admit you have needs.

If you're a leader and you want the people you serve to connect with you, to work as hard as you do, and to remain loyal, then you must be willing to open up to them at times. Admit your mistakes. Tell them your needs. Share what you're really thinking. People unify when their leaders are strong enough to share their weaknesses. Open your heart before you open your mouth, and you'll be amazed at what a difference it makes in your communication.

Beneath the Words

We must also learn to listen before we open our mouths to launch our messages. Often we simply nod and make a concerted effort to look like we're paying attention to others when really we're thinking about what we're going to say next, what we want to have for lunch, or what time we need to pick up the kids after practice. Instead, we need to listen beneath the words to the hurt that is in someone else's heart. You don't have to be a counselor, pastor, or social worker to realize how much people around you are hurting. No matter how great their lives may seem from your perspective, everyone hurts. If you listen beneath the words of those you love, you'll hear the hurt and connect with them on a deeper level.

Listening also means that you look into other people's eyes and try to discover what they really love, what their interests are, what they dream about. When one of my sons was about three or four, sometimes he would come to talk to me while I was reading the morning newspaper. He would immediately swat the paper down, gently grab my chin, and turn my face so I was looking right into his eyes. He wanted to make sure he had my full attention, because he wanted to be noticed, listened to, and understood.

My son is not alone. God created us with a longing to be totally understood. We want to be seen, not as the public persona who works hard to look successful and have it all together, but as we really are. We want someone who has looked into our heart—warts and all—and still loves us. Spouses, children, friends, team

members, and co-workers want us to respect them by giving them our full attention, our ears as well as our hearts. They want us to see them and still love them.

Make It Count Moment

*Do you consider yourself a good listener? Why or why not? What
prevents you from listening more closely to those you care about?
How closely do they listen to you?*

Truth Means Trust

As I've watched a number of people face the end of their lives, I've noticed how
motivated they are, finally, to tell the truth. When we remember that our days are
numbered, we realize we don't have time to waste on anything that's not true.

In relationships the stakes are just too high to beat around the bush, talk
behind someone's back, or not speak honestly. You gain respect when you speak
directly. Just as Jesus is "the Word...full of grace and truth" (John 1:14), we need
to be honest and up-front. In Patrick Lencioni's best-selling business book *The
Five Dysfunctions of a Team,* he concludes that in most workplaces today, people
don't speak the truth or share their true feelings. They may gossip, they may stab
others in the back, they may have strong opinions and hold them in and get bitter, but very few people speak the truth. Why? Because it's easier just to act nice
and say what others want to hear. Everyone acts pleasant because no one really
wants to share the truth from a gut level. Lencioni believes this tendency shows a
lack of trust in the organization.

Great relationships as well as great organizations are built on trust, and you
build trust by telling the truth. The more you tell the truth, the more you cultivate an atmosphere where everybody can be honest. This facilitates real communication, which in turn builds a great business, a great family, or a great marriage,
because all great things are built on the foundation of trust. Ephesians 4:15 says,
"Instead, we will lovingly follow the truth at all times—speaking truly, dealing
truly, living truly" (TLB). We must be willing to tell the truth but also to temper
it with grace. When you're angry, you need to talk about it. When you feel hurt,

you need to talk about it. When you have a strong opinion, you need to share it. But how you share the truth can be just as important as the words themselves.

If you respect others when they speak truth, even if they tell you things you don't like about yourself, your decisions, or your actions, then they will know that you value them. Even if you disagree, the way you respond to them sends a message that either improves future communication or impairs it. The truth can be messy sometimes, but it always builds trust and strengthens the foundation of the relationship.

Break Through the Static

I am amazed by the technology of satellite phones. Using this small device when traveling, I am able to connect to a large satellite in space that then links me to my home in Houston. Even though we may be thousands of miles apart, I can suddenly hear my children's voices. There are times when we seem worlds apart from those we love, and we suffer because of the emotional distance. That's when God wants to bridge the gap. He wants you to call on Him so He can help connect you with the people in your life. He will open up their hearts. That's how Christ communicated with us, by connecting with His Father. I communicate so much better with the people in my life when I connect with my heavenly Father first. In fact, if you are married and you both grow closer to God, then you will grow closer to each other. The closer I grow to God and connect with Him, the satellite, the more clearly He emits a signal to the people I'm trying to communicate with. Maybe you're in a situation where a relationship is really breaking down and you don't know what to do. Call on God. Ask Him to open up that person's heart and to give you the words to say.

God tells us, "Call to me and I will answer you and tell you great and unsearchable things you do not know" (Jeremiah 33:3). When we call on Him, we never get a busy signal. He never puts us on hold. When we don't have the words to convey how we feel, when we have hard things to share that will hurt those we love, when we need to find the time and place to tell people how much they mean to us, we can ask Him for help. Be honest about it and ask, "God, give me the words to say to my wife to really show her how much I love her." "Lord, give me the words to say to my teenagers to really break through to them because it's hard right now." "Heavenly Father, help me know what to say to the friend I've lied to."

If your relationships aren't what you want them to be and if you need to work on communicating with the most important people in your life, God wants to help you. He will enable you to break through the static so you can hear each other's heart. All we have to do is ask. "But if any of you lacks wisdom, let him ask of God, who gives to all generously" (James 1:5, NASB).

True communication is about connecting, sharing, and understanding. If we really want to remove the accumulated armor that envelops us over the course of our lives, we have to be willing to risk our hearts and reveal who we really are. We must be willing to listen, identifying the unspoken needs of others as well as discerning their dreams. As you share the truth and ask God to open up the communication channels, your life will become rich in rewarding, transparent, strong relationships.

Make It Last for Life

1. Look through the speed-dial list on your cell phone. Of the people on your list, whom do you consider the most important? How often do you call them compared to the others on the list? How often do you really communicate with them?

2. Write a letter, send an e-mail, or call someone who's important to you but lives far away. Recall the last time you were together, and tell that person what it meant to you.

3. Try a twenty-four-hour media fast (no television, radio, computer, or newspaper) to help you tune out distractions and listen to the people in your life. After your media fast, write down how it affected you.

Learn

Humbly

Star Power

Discovering Who You Were Meant to Be

> Shoot for the moon. Even if you miss you'll be among the stars.
> —Les Brown

> There lives in each of us a hero awaiting the call to action.
> —H. Jackson Brown Jr.

I love to stargaze, to look up into the sky on a clear summer night and see hundreds, maybe thousands, of glittering jewels pierce the darkness. During these moments I'm reminded of how small I am and of how large God is, and I wonder why I matter to Him, why I'm not lost in the sea of seven billion people on earth just as Polaris, the North Star, blends into the twinkling lights of the Milky Way.

In one of his poems that we know as the psalms, David reveals that he had the same question. "When I look up into the night skies and see the work of your fingers—the moon and the stars you have made—I cannot understand how you can bother with mere puny man, to pay any attention to him! And yet you have made him only a little lower than the angels" (Psalm 8:3–5, TLB). Here's a very important person of his time, a man whom God selected from obscurity and anointed as the king of Israel, wondering why God made him. Basically, David said, "God, when I look at all that You've created, I feel like just a speck of dust.

Who am I and what is my place, what is my location, my niche, my position in the grand plan of life? Who have you created me to be?"

The answer to David's question is the same as God's response to us. God repeatedly and emphatically tells us, "You mean so much to me. I have a grand purpose for your life. I had a specific reason for creating you exactly as I did." He knows us intimately and doesn't lose us in the crowd, doesn't forget us or let us go, even when we may feel otherwise.

As we shift into this third section—Learn Humbly—we start with one of our most basic, ongoing questions: who am I *really*? Throughout our lives we continue to learn more about God's personality and His love for us, even as we also learn about ourselves. Whether we have four weeks or four decades of life left, we must be lifelong learners, changing and maturing through the many seasons, circumstances, trials, and triumphs.

So how do we discover who we were meant to be? Whether you're seriously asking this question for the first time or have been pondering it for many years, the starting point is the same. Just as an astronomer has to look through a telescope at the night sky to understand it, you have to take a closer look. First, you have to look up to the Source of your creation if you're truly going to comprehend who you are and what you were created to do.

Make It Count Moment

When was the last time you wondered about your identity and place in life? What were the circumstances? How did they influence your question?

Interior Designer

We are created in God's image, so it makes sense to look at His character in order to understand ours. In his letter to the Romans, Paul wrote, "For since the creation of the world God's invisible qualities—his eternal power and divine nature—have been clearly seen" (1:20). Paul makes the correlation between the creation and the Creator; when he looks around, he finds proof that there's a God.

In 1995 scientists pointed the Hubble Space Telescope into an empty patch of black space about the size of a grain of sand just above the handle of the Big Dipper. They wanted to test the clarity and range of the Hubble and were shocked when the pictures came back. That little patch of empty space wasn't empty at all. The pictures revealed over a thousand previously unknown galaxies. Scientists now estimate there are more than 125 billion galaxies in the visible universe. Each one of those galaxies contains millions of stars. It's mind-boggling! My little finite mind can't even begin to grasp such magnitude. If this is the size of only what we *know* of creation, then how much greater must the Creator be? How much power and imagination must He possess in order to craft such beauty, force, and complexity?

When you look at the complexities of creation here on this earth, it's evident that Someone is behind it all, an Intelligent Designer who created every bit of it. The more I learn about creation—whether it's the life cycle of a moth or the way my brain works—the more convinced I am that there is a Creator. Edwin Conklin, professor of biology at Princeton University, says that the probability of life originating from an accident is comparable to the probability of a dictionary resulting from an explosion in a printing factory. When we see the intricacy, beauty, and efficiency of creation, we know it couldn't have occurred by random circumstances. There has to be a Creator. Ironically, it takes a lot more faith to be an atheist then it does to believe in God.

If there's no Creator, then we're just here by accident, an arbitrary occurrence of nature. If we're on earth by random chance, then how can there be purpose in life? There would be no need to go any further in this book to understand our identity and purpose on this earth, because if there's no Creator, then there is no greater meaning, no larger purpose. We're just here to enjoy all we can while we can. So live it up, have fun, don't worry or look for meaning in your life because it doesn't exist. If there's no Creator, we're basically just a curious, self-aware kind of animal.

But the good news is that, because we see intentional fingerprints all over creation, there must be a Master Designer. The proof is right before us. It's like one of those three-dimensional drawings where you stare at the design a certain way until the hidden picture emerges. Some people can see the three dimensions instantly, and others of us struggle no matter how long we stare and squint.

When I look at creation, I see a Creator, and I also see what kind of Creator He is. I see His personality, His power, and His playfulness. I see how much He loves uniqueness and variety. Think about the duckbill platypus or a monarch butterfly. Or consider your own body. If you don't believe that God loves variety, just go to the nearest mall, sit on one of the benches, and watch the wonderfully diverse people walking by. We are the result of an amazing Imagination unlike any other.

Avoiding Identity Theft

So if we're His handiwork, created in His image, then why do we struggle so much to know who we are, to know our real worth? In the Disney classic *The Lion King*, once we move past all the circle-of-life stuff, the answer is illustrated powerfully. You'll recall the story of the young lion, Simba, heir to the kingdom, who's falsely blamed for the death of his dad, Mufasa. Simba runs off in guilt and fear and gives up on his dream of becoming king until one day out in the wild, Mufasa appears to him in a vision and says, "Simba, you have forgotten me." And Simba says, "But, Dad, how could I ever have forgotten you?" His father replies, "You have forgotten who you are, and therefore you have forgotten me. Remember who you are. You are my child, the one true king."

I love this scene because it reinforces such an essential truth about who we are. God says to you and me today, "Remember who you are. You are My child. You are a child of the King." Too many people today have forgotten their Creator, so they have completely missed out on the purpose and meaning of life. They're not really living; they're just existing. They don't know their place in life because they have forgotten whose they are, and therefore they have forgotten who they are.

Many times they've had help in forgetting, in losing sight of their true identity. In our hypertech computer age, we hear a lot about the perils of identity theft and how to avoid it. So we choose safe Web sites that use encryption and other safeguards against a hacker stealing our vital statistics and, with them, our identity. But identify theft is not a new phenomenon—in fact, it's one of the oldest in the book, our Enemy's number one strategy. He wants to steal your awareness of who you really are. While God's purpose is to bring you life to the fullest, Satan has a plan for you to settle for so much less than what you were made for. The thief's plan is to steal, kill, and destroy. He knows if he can steal your identity, he will destroy your dreams and your purpose in life. You and I need to constantly be aware that we are at the center of an epic battle. As C. S. Lewis put it, "There is no neutral ground in the universe; every square inch, every split second is claimed by God and counterclaimed by Satan."

Satan comes to us and whispers, "You're not valuable. God can never use you. In fact, God is ashamed of you because you've blown it. And blown it again and again and again. You're not worth much anymore. God has put you on the shelf because you've failed to live up to what He hoped for you. You're not talented enough. God uses other people, but He doesn't use you. God can't use you— you're not spiritual enough, you're not smart enough, you're not committed enough, you're not strong enough." Any of this sound familiar?

Our Enemy tries to undermine our confidence in who we're made to be. But God constantly says to us, "Remember whose you are. You are My child. You're a child of the King. That's your true identity. You're forgiven. You're righteous in Me. You are so valuable to Me. You are worth so much to Me that I came to this earth, and I died for you. That's how valuable you are. You're worth dying for. I love you that much."

Make It Count Moment

When have you experienced the Enemy trying to steal your identity? What are the messages that run through your mind when you're down on yourself? How can you counter these indictments the next time Satan throws them at you? In other words, in those moments how can you remember who you really are?

Making the Grade

After we realize and embrace the way our Creator works in deliberate, beautiful, and intricate designs, then we can turn and look at ourselves. We can direct the telescope back at ourselves and discover our true identities. We can realize how we're made to accomplish His purposes. "For we are God's workmanship, created in Christ Jesus to do good works, which God prepared in advance for us to do" (Ephesians 2:10).

To make this discovery and live in light of it, you must gravitate to your strengths. Donald O. Clifton, in his book *Living Your Strengths,* says from a very young age we are taught to be "well rounded." Our ticket to our teachers' approval is to soften our sharp edges, to become smooth and well rounded. According to Clifton, however, what we're often taught is how to become as dull as we can possibly be. We're taught to play it safe, to be compliant, to follow convention and tradition, to color inside the lines and to stay inside the box.

God never meant for us to be well rounded. He has gifted each of us uniquely, and no one has all the talent, no matter how it might appear. We're to focus on what we're good at and let go of what we're not good at. I am not a good singer—just ask anyone who knows me! I could spend all my time taking voice lessons and auditioning for *American Idol,* but I would only go from bad to lousy. Instead I've focused on the key areas in which God has gifted me, and I've tried to develop them. I'm always working at being a better writer and communicator. It's an insult to God when we focus on the gifts and passions we don't have and try to develop only our weak areas. Our greatest potential lies in the areas of our greatest strengths.

How do we begin to know who we are in life? No matter the stage we're in—student, young adult, single, married, new parents, empty nesters, seniors—we can all learn more about who God made us to be by focusing on Him. As we develop a closer relationship with God, we become more like Him, thwarting our Enemy's attempts to steal our identity. When we look to our Creator as the source of who we are, we can shine brighter than any star in the night sky.

Make It Last for Life

1. Tonight (or the next clear night) go outside and spend some time alone looking at the stars. Where does your mind go? Where does your heart go? Once you return inside, read Psalm 8. Now write your own poem to God, expressing your experience and including your own questions and longings.

2. This week find an object that reminds you of who you really are. It may be a picture of you doing a favorite activity or posing with loved ones. Maybe it's a rock from a hike or a piece of jewelry from your grandmother. Keep it with you or in a prominent place you will see every day as a reminder of your true identity.

3. Make a list of your strengths—everything you can think of. Make them as specific and concrete as possible, or provide examples if they tend to be general. Instead of saying you're creative, specify that you're a gifted watercolor artist. Now go back over your list, and beside each one write how much time this past week you devoted to using or improving that gift.

GPS

FINDING YOUR DIRECTION

> The place where God calls you is the place where your deep gladness
> and the world's deep hunger meet.
> —FREDERICK BUECHNER

> When I stand before God at the end of my life,
> I would hope that I would not have a single bit of talent left,
> and could say, "I used everything you gave me."
> —ERMA BOMBECK

*A*re you as grateful as I am that a GPS—Global Positioning System—has become available for in-car use? Maybe it's my *Star Wars* upbringing, but I appreciate the brilliance of the concept and love the convenience. From somewhere in space, satellites direct a signal down to this little device, which can then tell me where I am and how I can find my way to my destination.

I've never been more grateful for GPS technology than on a recent trip my family took to Sweden. When we arrived in Stockholm, we rented a car with a GPS system because we had meetings scheduled that would require us to travel all around this city of a million-plus people. So coming out of the airport, I handed the GPS to my teenage son, Ryan, to program since I had no clue.

In a matter of moments, we were well on our way, guided by a confident automated voice telling us, "Turn left in fifteen kilometers," or, "Turn right in eight hundred meters." Everything was going great until we hit downtown and apparently lost our satellite signal among some tall buildings. Our directions became intermittent, so I made several wrong turns until we were, in short, lost.

Finally, with a little help from Ryan, we discovered that, when placed on the front dash, the GPS can always pick up its signal. After our slight delay, it guided us smoothly to our hotel. In life we need a clear signal from God so we can discover our position and place in the world. Until we discover our place, our niche, our purpose in life, we'll always feel lost, even when surrounded by a crowd.

Make It Count Moment

When was the last time you were driving and became lost? What happened? Did you stop for directions? What's your usual response when feeling lost, whether on the highway or in the circumstances of your life? Where do you turn for direction?

A Galaxy of Gifts

GPS isn't just for navigating between geographic locations. It represents a great way to consider what God has instilled in us to help us find the road to an abundant life. As we explored in the last chapter, our individual identity and unique purpose go hand in hand. If we want to know what we're called to pursue in this life, then we must look at how God created us. David wrote in Psalm 139, "I praise you because I am fearfully and wonderfully made" (verse 14). We know that we're made in God's image and that the value He places on us is inestimable. He was willing to pay the price of death and separation from His Son so we could be in full relationship with Him.

But practically speaking, how does this help us know how we should live and what our purpose is? We must be willing to activate the GPS that our Creator has installed in us. If we're going to find our way through the many circumstances and choices of life, we must be willing to use three crucial resources: our **Gifts**, our **Passions**, and our **Struggles**.

God has lavished on us a galaxy of gifts, and He didn't leave you out. He has provided you with unique abilities and talents. In one of his letters to the early church, Paul wrote, "There are different kinds of gifts, but the same Spirit. There are different kinds of service, but the same Lord" (1 Corinthians 12:4–5). Some gifts are the natural talents with which you're born, and others are the spiritual gifts that come alive when you commit your life to loving Christ. Paul makes the observation that the distinction really doesn't matter, because whenever you do something well and it brings honor to God, it's a spiritual thing. Whether they're natural talents or spiritual gifts, they're all from God, and He loves it when you use what He has given you. Some of us are good at speaking, others at singing. Some people are good at accounting, others at designing. Some at leading, others at teaching. Living here in Houston, I've learned that barbecuing is definitely a spiritual gift in Texas.

We're all experts at something, and no one excels at everything. Often we compare ourselves to others and become discouraged because we can't organize as well as they do, play sports as well, write as well, tell jokes as well. We overlook and minimize the gifts we've been given, because we're focused on what we don't have or can't do as well as others.

How do you discover what God has given you? Ask yourself what you do well and answer honestly. Ask your Creator, the One who made you. And ask your friends and family, "What do you see as my main gifts, my primary strengths? Where do you see my talents most clearly on display?" You must ask others, especially those who know you well and see you day in and day out, because when you're gifted at something, it may come so naturally that you don't recognize it yourself. You need someone else to hold up a mirror and point it out to you.

As you ask yourself, God, and others, don't slide into false modesty and self-righteous humility. "I'm not a good speaker. It's all God." While it's true that He is the source of all good things, we often hide behind such language as a way of avoiding the full responsibility of our gifting. Be honest with yourself about what you do well and how effectively you use that gift. How you exercise your gifts often depends on what you care about most, your passions.

God Within

We find our place and purpose in life when we discover our passion. Paul wrote in Romans, "Never be lazy in your work, but serve the Lord enthusiastically" (12:11,

NLT). The word translated as "enthusiasm" comes from two Greek words meaning "God within." Enthusiasm and passion come from God within us. He has placed the passions of my life deep inside me for a reason: He wants me to pursue those passions. If my gifts are the engine I'm given, then my passion is the fuel that packs a punch and keeps me going.

Too often people have the misconception that if they're passionate about something and gifted to do it, God probably doesn't want them to. Instead, they think He wants them to prove how much they love Him by giving up their talents and dreams and doing something they hate, something that they find difficult, boring, and tedious. That is ridiculous and often just an excuse to justify their lack of focus. God has given you gifts because He wants you to use them. God has given you a passion for something, and He wants you to develop and pursue it. Do you have a buried gift? Maybe it's something you loved to do but gave up to get a "real job." Never give up on something that you can't go for a day without thinking about. It's not too late to become who God created you to be.

So how do you discover what your true passion is? Ask Him. Pay attention to what you enjoy doing. Take note when you find yourself caught up in the joy of an experience, whether it's gardening or teaching, running or baking. When you enjoy doing something, the time flies and your emotions with it. It may be hard work, but your love of the thing transcends the sweat and effort. Living in the midst of what you're passionate about will also delight God. As Eric Liddell says in *Chariots of Fire,* "When I run, I feel His pleasure." You'll have a sense of pleasing God because you'll know that you're doing what He created you to do. You will be fulfilling the potential of the abilities with which He's gifted you.

Recently I took my two teenage sons and a couple of their friends to an amusement park in Dallas. Maybe I'm getting older, but I'm just not as passionate about riding roller coasters as I once was. Besides, they don't make 'em like the Big Dipper anymore! Between the bruised ribs from being slammed around hairpin curves at breakneck (I gained a new appreciation for that word) speed and the nausea from a thousand-foot drop, I wondered what I was thinking when I suggested the trip.

My sons and their friends, on the other hand, couldn't get enough. They were all saying, "Man, I about hurled! I thought I was going to pass out. It was awesome! Let's do it again." Apparently we had similar experiences but vastly different responses. The next day when I woke up, my head was killing me. My neck hurt,

I was stiff, and I was limping—I felt awful. As I asked myself, *What was I thinking?* the answer came quickly. I'm no longer passionate about riding roller coasters, but I am passionate about my kids.

Because I'm passionate about my kids, the entire experience—aches, pains, bruises, and all—was more than worth it. My intense joy came from watching my kids revel in the experience. Watching the smiles on their faces when they were just about to throw up was unbelievable. I loved it because I love watching my kids do something they are passionate about.

God feels the same way about you. When you pursue the passions He has placed in your heart, He simply loves it. When you're smiling and enjoying life to the fullest, your Father beams. He finds so much joy in your living out your giftedness and being who He created you to be. We not only feel fulfilled as we live from our passions, but we sense God's pleasure as well.

Make It Count Moment

When was the last time you felt passionate about an experience? What were the circumstances? What gifts did you use? What does this experience tell you about your purpose in life?

Total Eclipse

It makes sense that our gifts and passions help us find our way and fulfill the abundant lives God wants for us. However, the third force in our GPS—struggles—is every bit as important as the other two. Not as pleasant perhaps, but just as significant. Why? Because when God allows us to go through struggles, problems, and difficulties, we learn to depend on Him. We learn our own limits and are reminded to look to Him for what we need most. As we learn to depend upon Him, He fills us with His power and His strength.

If we never had any struggles or problems, we would never depend on God and would miss out on knowing what it feels like to have His power in our lives. Not only do our struggles help us rely on Him, but they also help us see what He wants us to do and, in the process, to find our way in life. Being the creative God that He is, our Father always uses our wounds to make us stronger and to help those around us. "He comes alongside us when we go through hard times, and before you know it, he brings us alongside someone else who is going through hard times so that we can be there for that person just as God was there for us" (2 Corinthians 1:4, MSG).

God allows problems and struggles into your life so you can come alongside others and help them. Many times it's the very struggles I'm embarrassed about that God wants to use to make a difference in others' lives. If I'll admit them and share them with someone who is experiencing the same thing, God can take my struggles and turn them into stars. God has created you to shine brightly—to be a unique star that shines for His glory. But the problem is that often we're eclipsed by others' expectations. Instead of being the bright star, the unique star God designed us to be, we succumb to false expectations based on our comparisons of ourselves to others. We conform. We people please. We strive for approval and settle for the path of least resistance rather than the abundant life of fulfilling our God-given destiny.

By providing you a GPS system, God has equipped you to avoid the detours and dead ends of the conformity trap. You have creative license to be who God made you to be. The great theologian Dr. Seuss once said, "Be who you are because those who mind don't matter and those who matter don't mind." Our greatest pleasure in life often comes from serving others, from giving them what no one else can provide in that exact time and place, whether it's a hot meal, a kind word, a listening ear, or a strong shoulder. We must be willing to be guided by the One who knows us best.

Make It Last for Life

1. On a piece of paper, number from one to five, and list five different gifts you know you possess. Don't be modest or shy; no one has to see this but you. This week ask at least three close family members or friends to list five gifts they see in you. Have them give you their lists so you can compare. What surprises you most? Why?

2. In what ways does your current job or career field reflect your passion? If you knew you only had a limited amount of time to live,
   would you want to continue in this line of work? Why or why not?
   Make a list of the obstacles that you believe prevent you from having
   your dream job or career. Go over these obstacles with God in
   prayer, keeping in mind that with your Father—the One who
   created you and knows you best—nothing is impossible.

3. Think through the handful of people who have helped you most in
   your life. How have their struggles, disappointments, and trials bene-
   fited you? What did they share of these experiences that made you
   stronger? Now prayerfully consider sharing one of your struggles
   with someone this week as a means of encouraging or motivating
   that person.

Hurricanes

WITHSTANDING THE WINDS OF CHANGE

> All I have seen teaches me to trust the Creator
> for all I have not seen.
> —RALPH WALDO EMERSON

> If you don't like something, change it.
> If you can't change it, change your attitude. Don't complain.
> —MAYA ANGELOU

The worst natural disaster in our nation's history blew in as a category-four-plus hurricane battering Galveston, Texas, on September 8, 1900. Winds estimated at over 140 miles per hour and tidal surges of sixteen feet slammed the island. More than six thousand people lost their lives, and more than thirty-six hundred homes and buildings were destroyed. Residents were clearly unprepared for the fury of what would later be called the Great Storm.

After such life-altering devastation, residents of Galveston made some radical changes. They built a sea wall seventeen feet high and three miles long to protect the area. With sand bars and ground-soil engineering, they also raised the elevation of the entire city by several feet. So when a storm of equal strength hit the island just a few years later, minimal damage was incurred, because the people were prepared.

When the hurricanes of life hit us, we must choose how we respond. Too often our relationships are blown apart because we're completely unprepared for the storms and stresses that come into our lives. We get pounded by an unexpected tragedy or crisis that blindsides us. We can't prevent the hurricane winds of change from blowing into our lives, our marriages, our families, our relationships, and our careers. But we can prepare for them and learn from prior storms. And storms will come—sooner or later. The only permanent thing in life is change. The Bible reminds us, "To everything there is a season, a time for every purpose under heaven" (Ecclesiastes 3:1, NKJV). Change is just a part of life.

The winds of change will either make you stronger or knock you down. In marriage the problems and trials will either draw you closer together or destroy your relationship. In your body, illness and injury can destroy your spirit or make you stronger than ever. In your career, a lost opportunity can snuff out your dream or inspire you to fan the flames more vigorously. It all depends on your response.

Winds of Change

As we've seen, the Bible addresses all aspects of what it means to be fully alive. Surviving the hurricane winds of change in life is no exception. By putting biblical principles into practice, we'll see that we can not only survive the winds of change, but we can harness them to fill our sails and propel us forward. Paul, a prisoner on a ship headed for Rome, describes a perfect storm of biblical proportions: "Before very long, a wind of hurricane force, called the 'northeaster,' swept down from the island. The ship was caught by the storm and could not head into the wind; so we gave way to it and were driven along" (Acts 27:14–15).

When the ship first encountered the hurricane-force winds, the crew tried to fight it. They tried to sail into the storm, perhaps to find the calm center, but soon they realized the futility of their efforts. It's hard to stop a storm in progress. Change is inevitable, and you can waste a lot of time and energy trying to fight it. If you don't learn to adapt to life's unexpected situations and move along with them, your ship will be destroyed. In the midst of life's worst blows, you can be tempted to cling to the past and romanticize the way things used to be. We all know people who just can't adapt to change. The wind shifts direction, and they scramble for security. They get stubborn and think back on how much better it used to be in the good ol' days.

The reality is that if we don't learn to adapt to the winds of change, we'll never enjoy life. Change is frightening, uncertain, and threatening, but it can also be healthy, dynamic, refreshing, and necessary. We must embrace the facts that life is a voyage and our ship will encounter storms at times. Remaining in denial, attempting to control, or clinging to the past will never fulfill us. Life is not found in navigating around the winds of change; the abundant life is found *in* these life changes. Alfred Souza observed, "For a long time it had seemed to me that life was about to begin—real life. But there was always some obstacle in the way, something to be gotten through first, some unfinished business, time to still be served, a debt to be paid. Then life would begin. At last it dawned on me that these obstacles were my life."

Make It Count Moment

What do you consider the happiest season of your life? How often do you think about it or find yourself wishing you were back in it? How does your present season of life compare to it? Is nostalgia causing you to miss out on present opportunities?

Crash Course

Learning and growing through life's storms require two key navigational tools. Sea captains encountering storms on the open ocean know that they can steer against the storm or steer with it. Most learn quickly that steering against hurricane winds can snap the ship's mast like a twig and crush the rudder with pounding waves. Usually it's better to steer with the storm, picking up speed at a frightening pace in order to avoid capsizing. We have to do the same and rethink the way we perceive the storm we're experiencing.

Paul was no stranger to this. For fourteen days he and his shipmates were surrounded by such driving rain and inky skies that they had no stable landmarks by which to navigate. "When neither sun nor stars appeared for many days and the storm continued raging, we finally gave up all hope of being saved" (Acts 27:20). They began to lose hope, because they couldn't see through the storm. You probably know the feeling. The storm has been raging in your life, and dark clouds have been swirling around you for days, weeks, or years. You're on the brink of losing hope because you can't see anything through the storm—nothing to help you get your bearings. If you are about to give up, don't! As Winston Churchill put it, "If you are going through hell, keep going."

We can learn from Paul's example as he remained calm in the midst of the crisis. He was the only one on board who stayed confident, because he chose to look beyond the storm. He could see beyond the raging waters and gale-force winds to an upcoming, positive change. Human nature inclines us to look only at the immediate problem and its collateral damage rather than any potential positive outcomes. We become negative, depressed, and desperate to escape from our pain and discomfort rather than looking beyond to the long-term effects. Often we blame God and become bitter that He doesn't immediately alleviate our situation.

God doesn't cause the painful changes in our lives, but He uses them and wants to bring good out of them. One way He does this is by growing our character. Psychologist John Townsend says immaturity is demanding that reality adapt to you. In the storms, immature people think, *If reality goes my way, then I'm really happy, feeling great. If reality doesn't go my way, I'm miserable, and I will let everyone know it.* Maturity, on the other hand, adapts to reality. And it's never easy. We're forced to acknowledge our weakness, set aside our way of doing things, and get in sync with a different, sometimes jarring, rhythm. Believe me, I've learned this the hard way.

A couple of years ago my family took a trip to Italy. We traveled all around the country by train and quickly realized that the Italian culture has its own timetable. Trains didn't always leave on time. Or arrive on time. In fact, they rarely did. Not surprisingly, no one in the transportation industry jumped when I wanted them to get organized and get their act together. My frustration simmered until I finally boiled over one afternoon. After our stay in a quaint hotel in a small hill town in Italy, we packed up and got ready to catch our train. We had reserved seats weeks ahead of time for the train scheduled to leave in two and a half hours. Being used to traveling with four children and lots of luggage, I had learned that planning ahead is critical. So I called the local cab company and explained that we needed a cab soon.

The dispatcher said in broken English, "Why are you calling now?" I confidently replied, "Because I need to book a cab now. There are six of us, and we have to leave in two hours. I just want to make sure your cab arrives in time for us to get to the station and board our train." As I was explaining, she cut me off with "Call us back when you need a cab" and hung up.

I nervously waited an hour and called again: "I need to book a cab in an hour. Please come to the hotel in one hour." With irritation in her voice, she curtly said, "Don't call now. Call back when you need the cab!" Finally, ten minutes before I needed the cab, I called back. She said, "Sorry, all the cabs are taken." I lost it right then. It was definitely not my proudest moment. I was so utterly frustrated with their Monty Python manner of doing things. Needless to say, we missed the train. However, this proved to be a turning point in our trip. We realized that we had to change the way we were viewing our time there. We finally accepted that we weren't going to have any success changing the Italian culture, and we reluctantly began to relax and go with the flow. We'll get there when we get there. Maybe they don't have everything running on schedule as we would like, but perhaps they know something about a more natural rhythm of pacing each day. The Italian culture didn't change; we did. We adapted and felt like locals by the end of the trip— one of our best memories and most valuable vacations ever.

Cargo Hold

Reality necessitates that we change how we view the world. Perspective can also help us clarify our priorities. If you only had one month to live, you wouldn't need this book to tell you what to focus on today, but in our routines and ruts, we often lose sight of what matters most. Change can clarify our priorities and illuminate what's really important.

During Paul's storm-tossed journey, the cargo that had once been so important began to mean little when compared with losing their lives. In Acts 27:18, Luke recorded, "We took such a violent battering from the storm that the next day they began to throw the cargo overboard." The crew started unloading everything that wasn't tied down to lighten the load so the ship wouldn't sink. The very same cargo they were so careful to pack onto the ship—I'm sure "Fragile" was written on a lot of the crates—now came off in a careless hurry. What was deemed valuable just a few days before suddenly seemed worthless. Whenever storms blow into your life and your ship is being battered, you will be forced to reevaluate your priorities. One of the most important priorities will definitely rise to the top: your relationships.

Make It Count Moment

What tangible "cargo" have you lost in one of life's hurricanes? What cargo have you had to intentionally release in order to survive a storm? How did your priorities change as a result of losing material items?

The Unmovable Anchor

While we must learn to adapt and change course to ride out the storm, we also have to know when to drop anchor and stay fixed in place. In Paul's story, Luke wrote, "Fearing that we would be dashed against the rocks, they dropped four anchors from the stern and prayed for daylight" (Acts 27:29). You need an anchor that never changes: "Jesus Christ is the same yesterday and today and forever" (Hebrews 13:8). While everything else is changing around you, God never changes. He's the same God as He was in Bible times. He can work the same miracles in your life today, and He'll be the same God tomorrow. Paul was confident during the storm because he knew this truth and acted upon it. In Acts 27:23, he explained, "Last night an angel of the God whose I am and whom I serve stood beside me." God anchored Paul with His presence and continues to anchor us the same way, even if we don't have angels delivering the message.

When hurricane winds blow in your life, remember that He knows right where you are. Maybe it feels like He's nowhere near and you're all alone. Even when you don't feel His presence, God is still with you. He's behind the storm, in the midst of the storm, and beyond the storm, always there waiting for you, ever present.

Right now maybe the storms are beginning to swirl in your life as new clouds gather and the wind picks up. You're afraid. Angry. Depressed. Anxious. Can't see your way out. The storm may claim your cargo, even claim your boat—as it did with Paul. (All passengers survived though the boat finally crashed.) You may be seasick, wet, soul weary, and weak. But you're going to make it. God will see you through with the unmovable anchor of His presence.

Perhaps the entire reason you're reading this page right now is so you can be reminded that He's in the storm with you. "'For I know the plans I have for you,' says the LORD. 'They are plans for good and not for disaster, to give you a future and a hope'" (Jeremiah 29:11, NLT). No matter how devastating the storm, He will see you through it. With God as your navigator, you will know when to ride with the storm and when to drop anchor and stand firm.

Make It Last for Life

1. If you knew you only had one month to live, what "cargo" would you throw overboard? In other words, how would you simplify your life? What material goods would you give away, sell, or trash? What items on your schedule would be the first to go? What keeps you clinging to this cargo presently? Make an inventory of items that you need to toss in order to keep your ship sailing smoothly.

2. How has your faith sustained you through some of the storms in the past? With the most recent storm in mind, what did you learn from it about yourself? What did you learn about God? Spend some time in prayer, connecting with your Anchor, thanking Him for the ways He has sustained you and will continue to hold you firmly.

3. What storms are you facing in your life today? Are they making you stronger or blowing you apart? Remember, you don't get to choose what trials come into your life, but you do get to choose your response. What response will you choose today?

Metamorphosis

CHANGING FROM THE INSIDE OUT

> Make room for that which is capable of rejoicing,
> enlarging, or calming the heart.
> —GERHARDT TERSTEEGEN

> How does one become a butterfly?…
> You must want to fly so much
> that you are willing to give up being a caterpillar.
> —TRINA PAULUS

People who discover that their time is limited often make radical lifestyle changes. They give up workaholism and slow down the pace of their lives, spending time with loved ones, with God, and alone, reflecting on their lives. They relinquish the pursuit and collection of material possessions and finally enjoy the fullness of what they already have. They rediscover the simple pleasures of curling up by a fire with a good book or sharing a picnic in the shade of a huge oak tree on a summer day. Their physical condition may force them to slow down, but most welcome the opportunity to get off the hyperspeed treadmills that their lives had become.

If you only had one month to live, you would likely slow down and take a different approach to each of your remaining days. Several terminally ill people I've known have told me that, ironically, they eventually felt relieved by their prognosis. By forcing them to slow down and make radical changes, their bodies provided something their souls had been craving for a long time.

For most of us, the desire to slow down and change how we approach life is already there. In fact, you likely wouldn't be reading this book if you didn't want more from your life, from your relationships with others, and from your relationship with God. You feel the urgency to make the most of your life, but too often you distract yourself with busyness, or you focus on things that can't fulfill your deepest desires.

Our restlessness manifests itself as a dis-ease of the soul, a growing discontent that has reached epic proportions in our twenty-first-century society. We make much more money and enjoy many more conveniences than our grandparents did, yet most of us are not happier. We decide that a vacation will enable us to slow down, but when we arrive at our destination, we discover that we have forgotten how to relax. We have difficulty spending time alone. We don't know how to connect with ourselves, let alone those we love most.

Motion Sickness

Our schedules move at such a rushed pace that we begin to suffer from spiritual motion sickness, one of the key symptoms of chronic soul disease. And what's the first thing we do when we feel this motion sickness of our souls? We move even faster. We're always moving to the next big thing, trying to satisfy ourselves. Maybe it's a new house, a new car, a new spouse, a new relationship. Maybe it's the latest high-tech gadget with all the upgrades, the next trip to a new and exotic locale, the next lottery ticket.

These desires aren't necessarily bad, but what motivates them is troubling. The only place to remedy the restlessness in our soul is inside. In his letter to the Romans, Paul describes how we begin such a transformation: "Do not conform any longer to the pattern of this world, but be transformed by the renewing of your mind. Then you will be able to test and approve what God's will is—his good, pleasing and perfect will" (Romans 12:2).

In Paul's prescription here, the key word "transformed" comes from the Greek word *metamorphous*, from which we get *metamorphosis*, literally meaning "to be changed from the inside out." The secret to faith-filled maturity is to be changed from the inside out, a metamorphosis of the soul. Now, when I think about the word *metamorphosis,* I think about a butterfly. The caterpillar forms a chrysalis and begins the process of transforming into something beautiful with wings. It doesn't wait for something to change it; it changes from the inside out, becoming all that it's created to be.

Too often we wait on someone or something external to change us. We blame our spouses for not fulfilling us emotionally, our churches or pastors for not fulfilling us spiritually, our jobs for not fulfilling our sense of purpose. But the blame game only delays the inevitable if we're serious about overcoming our disease and having healthy, dynamic souls. It's time to take responsibility for our own growth. If you have to move one inch from where you are right now to be happy, you'll never be happy. Because wherever you go, there your discontented self will be. It's not about what's on the outside; it's what's on the inside. The antidote to the motion sickness of our souls is stillness, the ancient art of just being still. Does the caterpillar climb into the chrysalis and work really hard at becoming a butterfly? No, the caterpillar becomes motionless, and the transformation takes place.

Spiritual growth and transformation will never occur in your life until you finally get still, until you stop moving. Paul reminds us to "fix your attention on God" (Romans 12:2, MSG). You can't fix your attention on God while juggling. Psalm 46:10 says, "Be still, and know that I am God." If we get still before God, we become transformed. Consider the well-known verses from Psalm 23: "He makes me to lie down in green pastures; He leads me beside the still waters. He restores my soul" (verses 2–3, NKJV). Motion and commotion steal the soul, but stillness restores the soul.

Make It Count Moment

When was the last time you were still? When was the last time you turned off the television and just sat quietly for thirty minutes? When was the last vacation that you did not check e-mail or answer your cell phone?

Mission Control

With the powers of science, research, and technology, we gain new information every day about how to improve our lives, stay healthier, and advance in our careers. There's nothing wrong with this information; however, it can give us a false sense of security that we can control our lives. We expend a lot of energy trying to control our images and acting like we've got it all together so no one will know that we don't. We try to control our problems. We try to control our pain. We try to control other people, but they just won't cooperate, and it's so frustrating! If we could just control everyone and make them do what we want, the world would be a better place, right? But that's not the way life works, thank goodness. The quickest way to suffocate our souls is to try to control everything.

The antidote to the control-freak fever that we all experience is solitude, time alone to be silent with ourselves and with God. When we remove the distractions and come before Him in silence, He begins to restore our souls. During these times, we can be honest about how little control we actually have over our lives. We can express our concerns, worries, fears, and doubts and ask for His control to prevail in our lives.

Most of us aren't very comfortable being alone. Without the need for posturing and posing, we have to face up to who we really are. But if we truly desire soul healing and nourishment, then we must commit ourselves to regular time alone. "This is what the Sovereign LORD, the Holy One of Israel, says: 'In repentance and rest is your salvation, in quietness and trust is your strength" (Isaiah 30:15). If we stop trying to solve all our problems and to control everything, quietness will fill our souls with strength.

Comparison Compulsion

Another symptom of our souls' disease emerges when we feel compelled to compare ourselves to everyone around us in order to know who we are and what we're worth. We measure ourselves to see how we stack up, often using status symbols and appearance for our assessments. We look at what others are wearing, at where they're living, at what they're driving, at where they're working, at their kids' grades and sports accomplishments. When we use status symbols to determine our worth and identity relative to others, our souls will dry up.

If you elevate status symbols, then you're really trying to give the appearance of a healthy, well-balanced, successful life without the reality of it. You're trying to change from the outside in, thinking you will feel better about yourself on the inside if you change your settings and props on the outside. We think, *If I change my looks, if I change my house, if I change my car, then it's going to change me. Then I will truly be content.* Only one problem: it doesn't work.

Metamorphosis originates within. I find it fascinating that the coloring on a butterfly is not caused by pigment but rather by a prismlike effect as light is reflected off its transparent wings. Despite the variety of colors and patterns, beneath the arrangement of their wing designs, all butterfly wings are transparent. Similarly, in our lives, transparency transforms. When we get real with God and others, when we're being who God created us to be rather than trying to pretend we're someone else, then our distinct individual beauty emerges.

Interestingly enough, the opposite of metamorphosis is the Greek word *metaschematizo,* meaning "to change the outward appearance." It's the origin of our word *masquerade.* Too many times we masquerade like we've got it all together when we are hurting deeply in our souls. God says we need a metamorphosis, not a masquerade. Real change is initiated on the inside; then the outside naturally changes to reflect it.

The best antidote I know for comparison compulsion (or status-symbol syndrome, as it's also known) is service. Not serving just anyone, but serving people who can't give you anything of value in return. Networking is an essential part of our communities and business relationships. But when you give of yourself to someone who can't repay you, then you cut through all the boundaries and connect more fully. It's no longer about comparison but about compassion.

Make It Count Moment

Presently, what person or persons are you serving who can offer you nothing in return? Who in your life needs you but may not be able to reciprocate? What prevents you from giving of yourself to them?

Crisis of Comfort

Often our goal in life is to be comfortable. Yet when our commitment to comfort affects our pursuit of God, we become stagnant, bored, and depressed. The final symptom of soul sickness in modern life emerges when we try to insulate ourselves from pain, suffering, inconvenience, and discomfort. The comfort-zone virus will steal our happiness and shrink our soul.

Our spiritual restlessness will continue to increase if we're trying to avoid problems in life. Returning to Paul's insight from Romans, we're instructed, "Base your happiness on your hope in Christ. When trials come endure them patiently" (12:12, Phillips). Notice that Paul doesn't say "if" but "when." Every single one of us will encounter trials in life. Most likely, you're in the midst of some challenges right now. And as you look ahead, more trials are probably right around the corner. It doesn't matter if you're young or old, wealthy or poor, on a farm or in a metropolis; suffering is part of life. No one is exempt from tragedy. No one is exempt from problems. The key is to remember that at the center of every problem is a purpose, a revelation of God at work in our lives. Our strength grows as we lean on Him during our struggles.

I'm reminded of a little boy who found a chrysalis on a branch. He thought it was moving, then saw that a butterfly was struggling to break through. He felt sorry for the butterfly, so he took out his pocketknife to help the butterfly avoid the struggle. He cut open the chrysalis, pulled out the butterfly, and held it in his hand, expecting it to fly away. But it didn't move, and within minutes the butterfly was dead. When the challenge to emerge from the chrysalis was removed, the butterfly's opportunity to strengthen its wings was denied. With only weak, wet wings, the butterfly was unable to survive. It needed to struggle in order to soar, and we also need struggles in order to soar. There is no way that we can be changed from the inside out without problems.

God allows trials in our lives because the only antidote to the comfort-zone virus is suffering. You don't have to go looking for suffering. Suffering will come into your life. Every one of us experiences deep wounds as we encounter tragedy, loss, and pain. I wish I could tell you that if you love God and pursue Him wholeheartedly, you'll never have a death in your family, never lose your job, never have a failed relationship, never get sick. But I can't say that, because suffering comes to all of us. The key is to recognize that God doesn't cause the problem, but He allows it in order to strengthen our wings so we can soar to our full potential. If we grumble and gripe, playing the martyr, suffering doesn't do anything for us, and our sorrows are wasted. But God doesn't want to waste a hurt; He doesn't want to waste a tear; He doesn't want to waste a sorrow. He wants us to endure with grace, and we do that by trusting Him.

Grace is the power to change—not what we can do for ourselves but what God does for and through us. When we become still and silent, when we start serving and embrace suffering in our lives, then we facilitate real spiritual transformation. We learn that we can't solve our problems in our own strength or alter our outward appearance and expect our lives to change. Metamorphosis comes only by grace. If you only had one month to live, you would want to stop the ceaseless motion of a busy life and find ways to enjoy stillness and solitude. You would want to nurture your soul by forgoing comparisons and instead looking for ways to love and serve others. You would want to find a way to suffer gracefully, trusting beyond what you can see and feel for what God promises. Many people are forced to try to make these changes all at once because their bodies fail. The good news is that you can begin today to alleviate the symptoms of your soul's discomfort and to rest in the healing balm of God's grace.

Make It Last for Life

1. Plan ahead this week so you can spend at least one hour alone and uninterrupted. Let others know you will be unavailable for calls or e-mail, that you'll be unplugged and inaccessible. If necessary, go where you will not be disturbed. Take nothing to read, write, or listen to. Just spend some time being still. You might stare out the window, take a walk in the woods, or remain quietly in your office after hours.

2. In what ways have you recently tried to change by altering your outward appearance or circumstances? Think of one change that you

could make in your schedule or lifestyle to allow yourself regular
time alone with God.

3. Think through the people in your life right now. Choose one new
   acquaintance to befriend, someone who needs you more than you
   need them. Look for a way you can serve this person.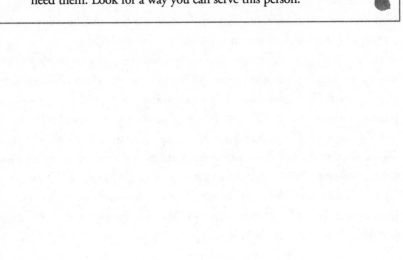

Earthquake

BUILDING A FOUNDATION THAT LASTS

God whispers to us in our pleasures,
speaks to us in our conscience,
but shouts in our pains;
it is His megaphone to rouse a deaf world.
—C. S. LEWIS

Pain is inevitable, but misery is optional.
We cannot avoid pain, but we can avoid joy.
—TIM HANSEL

One of the most difficult lessons in life is how to accept loss. And it's an ongoing process since our lives constantly change and we're forced to confront the harsh realities of a world that's far from perfect. Whether you are single or married, a teacher or a student, a business executive or a stay-at-home mom, you have most likely faced some moment when your world was shaken to its foundation. The marriage that seemed unbreakable. The parent who exercised every day. The business that succeeded beyond your wildest dreams. Suddenly a divorce, a heart attack, a bankruptcy created seismic waves that resulted in enormous collateral damage.

During these times, our faith can be shaken to the core. On one hand, such trials and painful losses force us to depend on God—for comfort, for peace, for His love and mercy. But on the other, we may become angry and resistant to Him because we can't imagine why He would allow such a tragedy, loss, or catastrophe in the first place. It's hard to fathom that our freedom of choice comes with one of the steepest price tags imaginable: the sorrow and anguish of an imperfect world. But God never abandons us. He suffers right along with us and knows more than anyone what it means to lose a child, to be rejected by His people, to be betrayed by a friend. In fact, look at what Jesus says: "In this world you will have trouble. But take heart! I have overcome the world" (John 16:33). Jesus said problems are a natural part of life, but they don't have to level us.

If we only had one month to live, we would want our lives to withstand the impact of such news and to provide a lasting foundation for all those we leave behind. The only way to do this is to intentionally strengthen our foundation each day, turning to the Master Builder for instruction and guidance in building our lives.

Rock Solid

When the earthquakes of life hit, we find out what we're made of and what we've structured our lives upon. Are we living with a false sense of security as we stand on the surface of underground fault lines? Will even the slightest seismic activity leave us in the dust?

None of us would dispute that a solid foundation is the key to a building's integrity, its structural strength from top to bottom. An unshakable foundation is also the key to building a meaningful life, a lasting marriage, a strong family, and a successful business. Jesus uses this common-sense truth to illustrate our need for a supernatural foundation that can withstand any disaster or tragedy we encounter: "Everyone who hears these words of mine and puts them into practice is like a wise man who built his house on the rock. The rain came down, the streams rose, and the winds blew and beat against that house; yet it did not fall, because it had its foundation on the rock" (Matthew 7:24–25).

Families today are collapsing left and right because they're built on unstable ground. You can't predict when an earthquake will come into your life, but Jesus says you can earthquake-proof your life by building on the right foundation. He says the way to do that is to put His words into practice. According to Jesus, the secret is not how much of the Bible you know; it's how much you live out His truth on a daily basis. How genuine is your faith? If you exercise it daily, when the earthquake comes, you'll be prepared to endure and emerge even stronger on the other side. Scripture reveals the secrets of putting God's Word into practice and establishing an indestructible foundation.

First, you need a solid center in your life. In Matthew 22:37–39, Jesus reveals this solid center in the Great Commandment. "'Love the Lord your God with all your heart…' This is the first and greatest commandment. And the second is…'Love your neighbor as yourself.'" It is so easy in marriage to look to your spouse to be the source of your happiness, to meet your deepest needs for fulfillment and purpose and meaning. But no human is equipped to sustain someone else at that level. When you look to your mate to meet needs only God can fulfill, you put too much pressure on that person and on the relationship.

If you have anything other than God at the center of your life when the earthquake of problems hits—and it inevitably will—your center won't be strong enough to hold you together. If you have a solid center, you have a solid life. A weak center, and your life crumbles. If you feel like your life is breaking apart, then you need to stop and examine what's at the core of your life. It's never too late to ask God to be the center of your life and to build upon His truth as your sure foundation. No matter how much the earth shakes and rolls and relationships and businesses collapse around you, with God as your unshakable base, you will stand. "In everything you do, put God first, and he will direct you and crown your efforts with success" (Proverbs 3:6, TLB). God wants to be the foundation for every area of your life: your marriage, your family, your business, and your finances.

Make It Count Moment

What does your life revolve around right now? Who or what is at the center of your life's wheel? Your family? Work? A dream? A goal? In what ways has this center sustained you? In what ways has it left you susceptible to circumstantial tremors?

Community Watch

Another primary practice for securing your foundation is having a community that cares, a human support system. You need a team of people around you who love you for who you are and not for what you do. You need some friends in your life who will walk in when everyone else walks out. How do you know who your friends are? When you go through a tough time, they are right there with you. They don't hang around only when everything is going smoothly. You have some acquaintances in your life that you may refer to as "friends," and you probably think of them fondly and enjoy being around them. But when the tremors begin, acquaintances cannot withstand the shaking. They take off and leave you standing in the rubble. Real friends walk in and catch you when times get tough.

God designed a way to meet this need we all have for community: the church. When one person or family experiences an earthquake, the rest of us gather around and help them remain strong, assist them in rebuilding, and take care of them. You need a support system because no one can make it in life all alone. "Two are better than one.... If one falls down, his friend can help him up. But pity the man who falls and has no one to help him up!... Though one may be overpowered, two can defend themselves. A cord of three strands is not quickly broken" (Ecclesiastes 4:9–10, 12). God designed us to live in community, gladly offering help when others need it and gracefully accepting help when we are in need.

Make It Count Moment

Who has consistently encouraged, challenged, and caught you? If you only had one month to live, what would you want to tell them?

Storm Shelter

When you face unexpected earthquakes, never forget that you have a shelter in the storm. You can run to the source of that peace that surpasses our understanding. God tells us, "Call upon me in the day of trouble; I will deliver you" (Psalm 50:15). God wants you to turn to Him first when trouble hits. But we try to solve all our problems, and then, as a last resort, as our lives begin to crumble around us and our resources are exhausted, we finally turn to God and say, "Well, I guess there's nothing left to do but pray!"

But this formula is backward; prayer should be our first response, not our last resort. God says, "Turn to Me first, pray about it, because I'm right here with you." How do you know if God is truly the center of your life? You stop worrying! Whenever you start worrying about something, it's a signal that God's been pushed out of first place, and something else has supplanted Him as the center of your life. Whenever you put God first in an area, you stop worrying about it. If God's not first in your marriage, you worry about your relationship. If He's not first in your finances, you fret over your bank account. If God's not first in your business, you can't sleep at night for thinking about the office. Whenever we begin to worry, we've lost our shelter and exposed ourselves to the elements that can shake our faith.

As long as you have a pulse, you will have problems. But I can tell you this: Jesus Christ will walk through every problem with you, and He will never let you down. Look what David said in Psalm 94: "If GOD hadn't been there for me, I never would have made it. The minute I said, 'I'm slipping, I'm falling,' your love, GOD, took hold and held me fast. When I was upset and beside myself, you calmed me down and cheered me up" (verses 17–19, MSG). You may be in the middle of the biggest earthquake of your life right now, and you're being shaken to your very foundation. You know you didn't cause it, and you're wondering why God allowed it. You may never know the answer on this side of eternity. But if you're committed to loving and knowing God, if you've entrusted your heart to His Son, then He will hold you in His arms and never let you go.

Our initial reaction when faced with a challenge is usually, *God, get me out of this situation. I need a miracle here. God, solve this problem, and hurry!* But God often responds to us with His presence instead of His presents. He says, *I'm not going to deliver you right out of it. There's no magic button or instant solution. Here's My plan: I'm going to hold you, and I'm going to walk you through to solid ground. I'm here with you when the earth shakes and when all is well.*

Singer Billy Joel was in California when he called his daughter in New York on her twelfth birthday and said, "Honey, I'm so sorry, but I can't be there on this really special day, but I sent you something really nice. I'm not going to tell you what it is, but your gift should arrive by late this afternoon. Be looking for it." Later that day his daughter heard the doorbell ring. She went out to the front porch and saw an enormous gift with a big bow on it. She couldn't imagine what it could be. She started opening it up and tearing into it and—Billy Joel himself came out! He surprised her. The best present she could have ever received was her dad's presence.

In the same way, God has already given you His greatest gift. I don't know what challenges you are facing in your life right now, but God does. He understands how you feel. He cries with you in your heartache, and He has the power to turn your life around.

Make It Last for Life

1. Describe the last time you experienced the tremors of an earthquake in your life—your most recent trial. In what ways did it challenge you and turn your life upside down? How are you different now because of it? Would you describe your faith and relationship with God as stronger or weaker in its aftermath?

2. Whom do you consider to be a true friend? Not just a friendly acquaintance but someone you could rely on in a crisis or heartache. If you are having trouble thinking of anyone, remember that the surest way to have true friends is to be a true friend. Who needs your help or encouragement today?

3. Make a list of the presents you would like to see God provide you. It might be a different job, a new relationship, or restored health. Spend some time considering what it means to long for God's presence more than any of these items.

Mulligan

PLAYING WITH INTEGRITY

> Guard the secret theater of your heart.
> See nothing there that you do not want to see happen in reality.
> —ROY H. WILLIAMS

> The difference between school and life?
> In school, you're taught a lesson and then given a test.
> In life, you're given a test that teaches you a lesson.
> —TOM BODETT

I f you only had one month to live, most likely you would want to review your life and examine your character. You would want to do all you could to learn from the mistakes in your past, iron out any wrinkles that had developed, and live your remaining days at peace. You would want your life to be integrated and whole, not compartmentalized and fragmented as we often experience when we're going through the motions of life and settling for less than we were made to enjoy. If you were living deliberately and passionately and were fully alive, you would want to live with integrity.

This word gets used a lot today, especially in political circles, but what does it really mean? The root of the word *integrity* is "integer." As you'll recall from math class, an integer is simply a whole number as opposed to a fraction. So integrity means wholeness as opposed to being fragmented and fractured in life. When you lack integrity, you end up acting one way at church and another way at work or at school. You act one way with your friends and another way at home with your family. A true sign of maturity and strength of character is to be the same person no matter where we are or whom we're with. Integrity is wholeness, consistency through and through. "Better to be a poor person who has integrity than to be rich and double-dealing" (Proverbs 28:6, God's Word).

As we see in this proverb, we can't put a price tag on integrity. When you have integrity, it fills your life with peace, passion, and purpose. When you are the same person at work and at church and with your family and with your buddies at the game or your girlfriends at the café, it fills your life with a calm unity. You're not always positioning and posturing, shifting and spinning, second-guessing who you should be in the various roles and settings of your life.

Sports seem to bring out both the best and worst in most of us. One of the places where integrity is the most evident to me is on the golf course. As an avid golfer, I can tell a lot about someone by playing eighteen holes with them. On the golf course, I can tell how competitive someone is, how creative, how honest, how well they handle adversity. I agree with John Wooden: "Sports do not build character. They reveal it." While the game of golf provides a pretty accurate mirror for a person's integrity, it also offers us some insights on how we can develop more integrity in our lives.

Complete Players

The pro golfers who win the most tournaments are the complete players. Consider Tiger Woods, for instance. He drives the ball a long way and drives it accurately. He also has a tremendous short game. He putts pretty well. Combine all of that, and you have the number one player in the entire world. He's a complete player. If you look at any of the PGA champions on any year's tour, you'll likely see that the winners are complete players. They may have key strengths in one area, but overall they have mastered the skills necessary to play well in all areas of the game.

Our personal integrity works the same way. If we want to live in an undivided, unbroken state of strength and peace, then we must be complete players. We must work to integrate our core values and beliefs into all we do, not just some of what we do. We have to be true to ourselves and to God in every area of our lives.

Many people, however, find it much easier to compartmentalize their lives and justify their inconsistencies. Consider a recent true story about a man and his girl-friend who went to a fast-food restaurant. They bought a bucket of chicken to take on a picnic, but the cashier mistakenly gave them a bucket full of the day's receipts. When they arrived at the park and opened their bucket, instead of drumsticks and wings, they found eight hundred dollars. The man immediately drove back to the restaurant to return the bucket of cash.

The frantic manager was so relieved when the couple walked in and returned the eight hundred dollars that he said, "Let me call the newspaper. We want to get your picture in the local paper because you are one of the most honest men I have ever met." The man quickly responded, "Oh, no, no, no." Then he leaned over and whispered to the manager, "I don't want our picture in the newspaper because, you see, this woman I'm with is married to someone else."

You can be really honest in one area of your life, but if you're dishonest in another area, you don't have integrity. You can be honest in four or five relation-ships, but if you're dishonest in one relationship, you don't have integrity. God wants us to be complete players, maintaining honesty, fairness, decency, and truth regardless of where we are or whom we're with.

Make It Count Moment

In what areas of your life are you most likely to cut corners or put aside your values? Relational? Financial? Spiritual? What part of your life is most challenging to integrate with the other parts?

One True Swing

In the golf movie *The Legend of Bagger Vance,* the mythical caddy of the title tries to help a washed-up golfer find his best swing. Bagger calls it his one true, authentic swing, found by playing on his natural strengths and compensating for his weaknesses. Every one of us has one true, authentic swing. But the problem is that we try to impress people. We're driving for show rather than trying to find our unique swing.

Performing to keep up an image and impress people requires tremendous energy and effort. It drains you of your true passion, diverts you from your God-given purpose, and robs you of personal peace. Frequently people suffer regret at the end of their lives because they know they have not lived consistently with their values and with the way God made them. They learn too late that the secret to passion is being true to God's design for them. You have to decide if you are going to try to impress people or influence them. Crowds are impressed by image, but you can influence people only by taking off your mask, being real, and admitting your faults and failures.

Integrity is the opposite of image. Integrity is when your private life matches your public image. When what you see is what you get—that's integrity. Integrity is who you are when no one is looking, when there's no one around to impress. When you're on that business trip and in a hotel that carries porn cable channels. When the salesclerk gives you back one bill too many. When the line on your tax return could be filled in so easily with a different amount. Integrity requires allowing your true character to take center stage and deciding to reveal who you really are and what you truly believe. "I know, my God, that you test the heart and are pleased with integrity" (1 Chronicles 29:17). God is pleased when we're complete players committed to honoring Him with our whole lives.

A Bad Lie

On long, hot summer days when I was a kid, my cousin and I liked to catch bees. Each of us headed out the door with an empty coffee can, complete with holes punched in the plastic lid. We would wander among the neighbor's gardens, eager to be the first to spot a bee hovering over the flowers.

The first bee was always an easy catch; it is nothing to trap one lazy, unsuspecting bee. The tricky part was capturing subsequent bees without letting the others escape. Clutching that humming, vibrating can made me feel powerful, but whenever I cracked open the lid, I sensed the danger within. Finally I would try to add one bee too many, and the angry swarm would emerge as I dropped the can and ran away as fast as I could.

Telling lies is a lot like catching bees. At first it's simple. Why not make things easier on yourself by stretching the truth a little? But one lie inevitably leads to others, because you feel compelled to conceal the original untruth. With each lie you add to the can, you risk releasing the others, and the can of lies you're forced to carry around gets increasingly dangerous. At some point, in the process of telling one more lie, they all escape, and your cover is blown, wounding you and stinging others in the process.

Many marriages fall apart because of a lack of trust. Partners don't trust each other because they lie to each other—about money, about other relationships, about their motives. Whether it's a business relationship or interacting with your children, if you demonstrate a willingness to lie, you will lose the other person's trust and may compromise the relationship for years to come.

How do you avoid the trap of a bad lie? The same way that you get out of a sand trap on the golf course. Golfers will tell you to open the club face before you hit out of a sand trap. In life you must open up and speak the truth. You don't hide from issues. You don't sweep things under the carpet. You don't stuff your true feelings. You speak the truth, the whole truth, and nothing but the truth.

When you tell the truth, it should be done lovingly, to build up the relationship and to help the other person, not to undermine or tear down. It's great to act like Simon Cowell on *American Idol*—someone's got to tell them they can't sing!—but only if you have the other person's greater good in mind. You share the truth not to hurt the person but to build the trust level and the strength of the relationship.

When you boil it all down, the real reason we lie is because we don't love enough. Lying is the easy route, a selfish convenience. It's taking the easy road, the path of least resistance for our own comfort. If you risk loving, then you'll tell the truth. The more you love, the less you lie. The more you love, the more you have the courage to tell the truth.

This also means having the courage to admit the truth about ourselves, to acknowledge when we've failed and need to ask for forgiveness. Especially regarding our own mistakes, the truth can feel unbearable—powerful, painful, and burdensome. We think, *If only I could choose again...* or *What if I...* or *Why did I...* But regret won't help us become people of integrity unless we transform it into repentance. We have to open ourselves to the truth on every front and operate from a position of honesty.

Make It Count Moment

When is it hard to keep your word? To whom? Your spouse? Kids? Co-workers? Parents? Friends? Others? In which relationships or situations are you most likely to find yourself in a bad lie? If you only had one month to live, who would need to be told the truth today?

Keeping Score

We must remember that God is the ultimate scorekeeper. At the end of my round of life, God will be there, holding up His perfect card as His standard of comparison. And ours will never match His; we are not holy, perfect, righteous, and blameless. He is. In life, there's only One who has walked this earth and shot an 18—a hole in one every time—Jesus. He lived the only completely integrated life. He never sinned. He never did anything wrong. He always did the things He should do. He never had a wrong thought or bad attitude. He was perfect.

Maybe you're shooting par in life, doing great things for everyone else, giving your time, energy, and money to those in need. But you still don't measure up to God. Your score is a long way from 18. And the truth is that we'll never reach 18, because we've all failed. The Bible says we have all made mistakes. We've all blown it in life.

God keeps the scorecard, and it's accurate. We're not going to come close to His perfect score. But here's the good news. Jesus gives us the ultimate mulligan, and if you're a golfer, you know a mulligan is a do-over. When you tee off and the ball slices into the woods, you can say, "I'll take my mulligan right here." Jesus gives us the ultimate mulligan because not only does He provide us a do-over, but He tees it up for us, and then He hits it for us. When He died on that cross more than two thousand years ago, He took my scorecard—all my bogeys, double bogeys, and triple bogeys—and He nailed that scorecard to the cross. He took my place. He does this for each of us if we're willing to accept the gift of relationship with Him; He replaces our scorecards with His.

Then with Jesus' perfect scorecard in hand, we face God as He welcomes us and celebrates our arrival into a place better than any winner's circle could ever be. "And what a difference between our sin and God's generous gift of forgiveness.... Jesus Christ, brought forgiveness to many through God's bountiful gift" (Romans 5:15, NLT). The good news is that because of the Cross we received the gift of a lifetime. We don't deserve it and could never earn it. But He loves us, simply loves who we are, no matter what we've done. He can restore us. He can make our lives whole, no matter how many pieces we're broken into or how few days we have left to live. He is the source of the integrated life we crave, the one we're made for.

Make It Last for Life

1. Take a sheet of paper and draw a large circle in the center of it. Divide the circle into a pie with eight pieces. Then label each section with an area of your life (for example, family, work, hobbies, marriage, finances, church, etc.). Are you living out your values in each of these areas?

2. Now draw a smaller circle in the middle of the pie, and write *God* in the smaller circle. This represents God's place in a life of integrity. God doesn't want a slice of your life; He wants to be the first part of every slice. Whether it's your hobbies or your marriage, God wants to be the first consideration in everything you do.

3. How would you rate yourself on the integrity meter? Are you the same person at home and at the office? with your family and your friends? Ask God to open your eyes to any areas you need to change and for the strength of character to do it.

Road Signs

EXPERIENCING A PERSONAL MIRACLE

> Miracles are a retelling in small letters
> of the very same story
> which is written across the whole world
> in letters too large for some of us to see.
> —C. S. LEWIS

> Attempt great things for God,
> expect great things from God.
> —WILLIAM CAREY

I've encountered hundreds of people who ask me how they can exercise faith during those hard, dry seasons of life when nothing seems to go right. Many of them say it would take a miracle for their lives to turn around—for their marriages to survive, their businesses to succeed, their kids to return. Talking with these folks, I always try to make two things clear: God is in the miracle business, and there's no formula or magic words. He's not a genie, here to grant our wishes. If you only had one month to live, the temptation might be to plead with God for a miracle to extend your life. And while our lives are clearly in His hands, and He can definitely heal physically, the miracle you truly need might have more to do with your priorities and relationships.

Maybe you're looking for a financial, physical, or relational miracle in your life. Miracles are not only possible; they're more common than we think. God cares for us and wants to work in our lives. The hard part is remembering this when we come to a crossroads and must choose how to respond. That great theologian Yogi Berra once said, "When you come to a fork in the road, take it." Not a lot of help. Whether we're facing a painful loss or confronted with choosing between two good options, the only way to experience the miraculous is to move in God's direction. There's definitely no formula, but in the Bible I find four road signs that can help us transform those forks in the road into a fulfilling, miraculous journey.

One-Way Streets

One of the best illustrations of these four guiding principles emerges from the Old Testament story of Elisha and the widow. Here we see the process God always uses when He wants to work a miracle in our lives. It begins with a dire situation and a plea for help: "One day the widow of one of Elisha's fellow prophets came to Elisha and cried out to him, 'My husband who served you is dead, and you know how he feared the LORD. But now a creditor has come, threatening to take my two sons as slaves'" (2 Kings 4:1, NLT).

On the heels of a terrible loss, this poor woman now faces an impossible situation. She has lost her husband, and because of this, she's in a financial bind. Creditors descend and threaten to claim her most precious possession in the world—her children—if she doesn't pay. She's in a quandary but reveals the first road sign in her response to the situation.

If you want God to work a miracle in your life, you have to realize there are two one-way streets you have to travel on to start the miracle. The first one is to admit your need. If you want God to work in your life, you have to admit that you need Him. Miracles never take place until you acknowledge the situation is impossible without God. Of course, we hate to admit it when we have a problem, much less acknowledge that we can't fix it ourselves. We would rather hide our troubles from others, pretend they don't exist, or try to manage them on our own. Often we complain about them, but that's not the same thing as being vulnerable about our inadequacy to solve our own problems. And yet God cannot work in our lives until we acknowledge that His intervention is essential and invite Him into the situation.

The widow in the story admits that she needs help. She goes down that one-way street, recognizing that no other road can take her to her desired destination. However, in Elisha's response, it appears that she hits a dead end: "Elisha replied to her, 'How can I help you?'" (2 Kings 4:2). His response seems pretty rude at first glance, as if he's frustrated that this woman is bothering him. But something else emerges here. I think Elisha was simply refusing to let her put her trust in him. He was saying, "Hey, I can't help you, but I know the One who can. I know the God who can work a miracle."

We can transform a defining moment into a miracle only by going down two one-way streets. The first one-way street—admitting your need—leads to the second one-way street—going to God as the only One who can lead you in the right direction. Where do you go when you have a problem? Do you call the psychic hotline or consult your horoscope? People try all kinds of things when they are in need, and it seems the more desperate we become, the crazier we get in looking to outside sources for help. There's only one outside source who can provide the miracles we need. We can go directly to God, the only One with the power, wisdom, and love to focus on our best interests.

Make It Count Moment

How difficult is it for you to admit your needs? What are the three greatest needs in your life right now? Who knows about them? What keeps you from sharing them with more people who care about you? What keeps you from turning them over to God?

Stop, Look, Listen

Now we're prepared for the next road sign on our journey—a stop sign. After his initial response, Elisha asks another strange question: "Tell me, what do you have in your house?" (2 Kings 4:2). God always asks this question before He works a miracle in our lives. Like the needy widow, we often get so caught up in what we don't have that we overlook the possibilities of what He's already given us.

God had already given this woman the beginnings of her miracle; she just didn't recognize it. We have to stop and assess what we have to work with. God always begins to work from where we are and with what we have; He doesn't just zap us and make everything peachy in one fell swoop. God asks, "Well, what do I have to work with? Stop worrying and start looking!" So you have to take everything you have and give it to Him. Your time, talent, resources, and energy, no matter how limited they may seem, are God's starting place. Your willingness and surrender activate God's intervention and blessings.

You-Turns Allowed

If you're going to see God transform your circumstances into His destiny for your life, you need to follow the third road sign and make a U-turn from a negative direction to a positive. Our first reaction when problems come our way tends to be negative. With sweeping exaggerations, we declare that everything is bad, nothing is good, and there's no hope.

This was the widow's initial perspective. Look at how she responds to Elisha's inquiry: " 'Your servant has nothing there at all,' she said, 'except a little oil' " (2 Kings 4:2). She starts out negative but quickly takes a U-turn to the positive. It would have been natural for this woman to have said, "Your servant has nothing there at all. Period. End of story. I don't have anything." But, instead, she turns it to the positive by adding, "except a little oil."

This shift in direction requires faith. She acknowledges there's one small resource, one ounce of possibility. In so doing, she exercises faith, which ignites hope. She's not in denial, but she's not willing to give up. Faith is not ignoring the present reality; it's acknowledging that with God all things are possible. It's not faith to pretend that a problem doesn't exist—that's either stupidity or denial. Faith doesn't deny the problem; it helps you see it from a new perspective, through God's eyes.

If you don't look through the eyes of faith, those small blessings will be overlooked, and you'll say, like the woman said at first, "There's nothing in my house. I have huge needs and serious problems. I don't see anything good in my situation." To shift to the positive and discover God's perspective, you must look through the eyes of faith. When you do, suddenly your attitude change provides room for God to work a miracle in your life.

God loves to take the little bit we have and multiply it, because then He alone gets the credit. God loves to take the ordinary and do the extraordinary, because in doing so He reveals more of who He is. Often we stifle His ability to provide the miracle even as we're praying for it. We become fixated on negative words, blaming others and worrying. None of these are conducive to faith or a shift in perspective. We can't recognize what God is doing in our lives if we're wallowing in our own negativity. We have to make that U-turn and focus on God instead of the problem.

Make It Count Moment

What's the difference between making a U-turn, as the widow in this story did, and being an optimist? How is seeking God's perspective more than simply looking for a silver lining?

Yield Ahead

The fourth sign on the road to a miracle is the most important one: the yield sign. If you follow the other three signs but don't follow this one, you can't expect a miracle. It's essential that we begin serving others with the blessings He's already given us.

In the widow's situation, Elisha asks her to do something very unusual. "Then he said, Go around and borrow vessels from all your neighbors, empty vessels— and not a few.… Then pour out [the oil you have] into all those vessels, setting aside each one when it is full" (2 Kings 4:3–4, AMP). Now this is a strange thing for the prophet to ask her to do. "Go out and borrow all the containers you can find." Strange, but apparently that is what God wanted her to do. And in fact, this is exactly what God asks us to do if we want a miracle in our lives. He asks, "What's in your house? What do I have to work with?" And then He quickly moves to "Look for empty vessels to fill."

This is just the opposite of my natural reaction to need. When I have a problem, my attitude becomes "I can't focus on anyone else's needs right now; I have needs of my own. I don't have time for anyone else; I'm overwhelmed and need to take care of myself first." My first inclination is to hoard the little bit of time, resources, and energy that I have. We are usually unaware of the empty vessels that surround us every day, because we're blinded by our own problems and worries. If you choose to look, empty vessels turn up everywhere: at work, in your family, in your neighborhood, in your church. Children are naturally empty vessels waiting to be filled with our time, energy, love, and attention. God asks us to give what we have, no matter how small it may be. He asks us to consider others before ourselves and to trust Him to take care of our needs and to be used by Him to meet the needs of others.

It's a paradox that we may never fully understand. When we move the focus off ourselves and onto God and start pouring our life into others and yielding to His direction, then He starts pouring His miracles into us. As counterintuitive as it may seem, the best advice I can give you when you're going through a problem is to look for empty vessels to pour yourself into. There is a certain logic to it. Why would God want to bless us if we're not willing to bless anyone else? We are blessed to be a blessing. When you move toward helping someone else, then He moves to help you. When you dig someone else out of their troubles, you find a place to bury your own. God waits to see if you have the faith to step out and start meeting someone else's needs and trust Him to meet your own. It's so unnatural that it's supernatural.

If you want to see miracles in your life, then find some empty vessels to pour your life into. Elisha tells this woman she has to take some action to get her miracle. She has to go out and get all the empty vessels she can find and bring them home. But look what happens when she does: "When the vessels were all full, she said to her son, Bring me another vessel. And he said to her, There is not a one left. Then the oil stopped multiplying" (2 Kings 4:6, AMP). Obedience brings blessing. The miracle God provides may not look like what we asked for, but ultimately we recognize how He has given us more than what we could have even imagined.

Somehow, someway, God works through our expectations. He works in our lives about as much as we expect Him to work in our lives. So what are you expecting God to do in your life today? God says, "If you will give Me the little bit you have, I can do great things through you." In Mark 10:27 we are assured that all things are possible with God. That includes anything and everything you're facing, right now, this very minute. But you have to admit you need help. You have to go to God, then make a U-turn from the negative expectations, and start looking to God and focusing on Him instead of your limitations. Yield to Him, and pour your life into empty vessels, trusting Him to provide what you really need. This is the road map for the life journey that you were made for, a life filled with miracles.

Make It Last for Life

1. Describe a time in your life when you experienced or witnessed one of God's miracles. How do you see these four road signs in the way God worked through that situation? As a reminder, the four signs are one-way streets (acknowledging our need and God alone as our provider), a stop sign (pausing to consider what resources we already have), a U-turn (from negative to positive in faith), and a yield sign (obeying God and filling those around us).

2. Think about one of your greatest needs right now. What resources do you have with which God can begin to work? Take stock of your life, and don't overlook the little bit of oil you have that may not seem directly related to your need.

3. Make a list of "empty vessels" in your life right now—people around you who need your input, resources, love, and attention. Whose need seems most urgent? Pray for God's leading, and look for a way to pour yourself into this person's life this week.

Sandcastles

CREATING A LASTING LEGACY

> The great use of life is to spend it
> for something that will outlast it.
> —WILLIAM JAMES

> Let's tell our young people
> that the best books are yet to be written;
> the best paintings have not yet been painted;
> the best governments are yet to be formed;
> the best is yet to be done by them.
> —JOHN ERSKINE

I love watching my kids make sandcastles whenever we go to the beach. Now that they're older, it doesn't happen as often, but they used to sit for hours, digging and smoothing, shoveling and patting, trying to get the turrets just right, making a nice wide moat and then filling it from the ocean with their sand pails. I remember when they were really small how shocked they would always be as the tide started to roll in. The waves would creep higher and higher until the foam began to lick the edges of their castle, and finally it was washed away. It took several attempts before my children realized their sandcastles were not permanent— they couldn't last.

Unfortunately, I've witnessed too many people at the end of their lives feeling the same way. They work nonstop, ever busy with a hectic, overbooked schedule. Then eventually their bodies force them to slow down and take a look at what they've struggled so hard to construct. The harsh reality they often face is that much of what they strove for won't last. After they die, it will wash away like a sandcastle at high tide.

As we begin the final section and focus on the principle of leaving boldly, it is so important to understand the investment required to leave a lasting legacy before it's too late. If you only had one month to live, you could make some changes that would improve what you left behind. But how much better to know that you're contributing to your legacy every day over many months and years and that all you're working for will last for eternity. The only way to create this kind of lasting legacy is to pour your most valuable resources into the investments with the greatest returns: people. Our relationships are the only investment that can't be destroyed by a fire or natural disaster or be lost in the stock market.

How many of us are using our resources to build a permanent foundation beneath our sandcastles? If we truly want to leave an eternally enduring legacy, then we need to look beyond our home, our investment portfolio, and our heirloom jewelry. If we're going to leave a legacy that the waves of time can't wash away, we need to do an on-site inspection of the life we're currently building. We must honestly evaluate the castle we're constructing to make sure it's not made of sinking sand.

The first aspect of this on-site inspection should be an influence evaluation. If I'm going to spend my time in such a way that I leave a legacy on this earth, then I have to pass the influence test. You may have more or fewer opportunities than I have, but we all have been given a limited number of opportunities to influence others and make a difference in their lives. God has invested in each of us the ability to influence others, and He expects a return on His investment. He wants us to take advantage of our opportunities rather than burying our heads in the sand and ignoring our responsibility to make a difference in the lives of others.

Sometimes people are more concerned with making a name for themselves than making an impact on others. They think, *If people know my name, then I'll be significant and fulfilled.* Abraham Lincoln wisely observed, "Don't worry when you are not recognized, but strive to be worthy of recognition." When we try to make a name for ourselves, it's like writing our names in the sand. The waves of time will eventually wash them away. The names of every rock star, movie star, pro athlete, politician, president, king, and queen will one day be forgotten. All those who are famous today will eventually be erased, because the waves of time just keep rolling in. They will wash away everyone's name, except for one—the name that's carved in stone, the stone that was rolled away. Philippians 2:10 tells us "that at the name of Jesus every knee should bow, in heaven and on earth and under the earth." My life, my time, is not my own. It belongs to Christ, and it's His name that will last; only when I live to influence others for Him will I leave an enduring legacy. You and I will be forgotten one day. Only what we do for God, how we fulfill the purpose for which He made us, will remain.

Make It Count Moment

For what would you like to be remembered? How are you contributing to this goal right now? How long will this legacy last?

Sand Dollars

Not only must we pass the influence evaluation to leave a lasting legacy, but we must pass the affluence inspection as well. If you're going to have an impact on eternity, you have to consider how you spend your material resources. You may be tempted to think, *Wait a minute, I'm barely getting by. I'm certainly not affluent! This must apply only to wealthy folks.* I understand where you're coming from, but with very few exceptions, if you're reading this book, you're considered affluent by the rest of the world.

Passing the affluence inspection is not as dependent on the amount of money you have as what you do with it. Jesus told a story about a guy who failed this test miserably. He was a businessman, and his barns were full, so he said, "I'll expand my business and be even more successful." Just take a look at the consequences: "'And I'll say to myself, "You have plenty of good things laid up for many years. Take life easy; eat, drink and be merry."' But God said to him, 'You fool! This very night your life will be demanded from you. Then who will get what you have prepared for yourself?' This is how it will be with anyone who stores up things for himself but is not rich toward God" (Luke 12:19–21).

God said, "No, you won't expand your business. It's over. You're out of here. The life you're building didn't pass the affluence inspection. I blessed you, and you used all the blessings on yourself. You failed the most important evaluation of your life." Every one of us has to pass the affluence inspection because God will one day hold us accountable for how we used the resources we were given.

There's nothing wrong with having resources and wealth as long as we realize that all the material things we have are just sandcastles. When children build sandcastles on the beach, they aren't devastated when the tide comes in and washes their work away. Kids don't sweat it; they just enjoy building the sandcastles. We should enjoy the material possessions God gives us but never get too attached to them or we'll be crushed when the tide of time takes them away.

The only way to pass the affluence test is by giving. We must learn to be givers rather than takers so we can make a difference. If we keep all that we own and earn only for ourselves, then we fail the affluence test. God wants us to be channels of His blessings, and if He finds that He can trust us, that we're obeying Him in this area, then He knows He can continue to bless us. On the other hand, why would God want to bless us anymore if we're just going to hoard everything He gives us? If we cling tightly to what He entrusts to us, then we become like the man building bigger barns. It's only when we gratefully use what He gives us to bless those around us that we build a storehouse of eternal treasure.

Make It Count Moment

Think about the possessions you will leave behind one day. Who will inherit them? Remember, we don't really own anything. We're just stewards of what God has given us.

Treasure Island

Finally, there's the obedience exam. Paul wrote in Ephesians 5:15–17, "So be careful how you live, not as fools but as those who are wise. Make the most of every opportunity for doing good in these evil days. Don't act thoughtlessly, but try to understand what the Lord wants you to do" (NLT). This may be the greatest secret to leaving a legacy of substance: try to understand what the Lord wants you to do—and do it. Obey God, because He gives you just enough time to do everything you need to do, both in your day and in your life. Note that He doesn't give you enough time to do everything that others think you need to do. To find out what God wants you to do, you have to spend time with Him and listen to Him, and then obey.

There are thousands of things we can do in life, but there are only a few things God intends for us to accomplish. When I live out His plan for me, everything falls into place. It seems as if He multiplies my time and I'm much more productive. Obedience always leads to God's blessing. When you use your influence and affluence to obey God, He will enable you to leave behind a permanent inheritance.

Make It Last for Life

1. List the three evaluations described here—influence, affluence, and obedience—and give yourself a grade on each one. In which area do you struggle the most? In which do you think you're doing well? What would your life have to look like for you to achieve an A+ in each one?

2. Review your calendar for last month. How much of your time was spent on temporary goals? How much on an eternal legacy? Look over your checkbook and credit-card statements. How much of your money was spent on temporary things? How much on eternal investments? Consider at least one way in the week ahead that you can invest in an eternal legacy.

3. Write your obituary. Start with what your life has been so far and then continue it well into the future. What do you want to be known for when you pass on? What legacy will you leave in your relationships?

Seeds

PLANTING FOR THE FUTURE

> The creation of a thousand forests is in one acorn.
> —RALPH WALDO EMERSON

> Faith is to believe what you do not see;
> the reward of this faith is to see what you believe.
> —SAINT AUGUSTINE

When I was growing up, my secret hiding place was high in the branches of a tree in our front yard. I loved to perch on its strong limbs and look out, camouflaged from the world. Still today one of my all-time favorite places to think is under a gorgeous, massive tree with leafy boughs stretching out to provide shade.

Some of the larger hardwood trees in our area were planted by settlers more than a hundred years ago. Apparently they had a vision for creating shady vistas in which their descendants could homestead or harvest the lumber to produce solid, stormproof homes. Considering that most of them never saw these trees reach maturity, the settlers' commitment to those who came after them is impressive.

As we think about what it means to make decisions as if we only had one month to live, the question remains: Is it possible to live in such a way that the impact of our lives is felt forever? I not only believe it's possible; I believe it's the kind of life we were made for. The Psalmist reveals how to live a life that outlasts you: "Generation after generation stands in awe of your work; each one tells stories of your mighty acts" (Psalm 145:4, MSG). With this truth in mind, let's look at the what, where, and why behind planting mighty oaks for eternity.

Make It Count Moment

What item represents an enduring legacy to you—a family home? your grandmother's ring? your family reputation? your favorite mountain? the ocean? something else?

Spiritual Gardening

It may seem obvious to begin with an examination of what you're planting, but its significance is still often overlooked. While we're all endowed with incredible gifts and opportunities, the type of seed we plant—and where we plant it—makes a huge difference in the kind of crop produced. Bottom line, it all comes down to the power of the seed.

In Matthew chapter 13, we find Jesus telling the parable of the sower: "A farmer went out to sow his seed. As he was scattering the seed, some fell along the path, and the birds came and ate it up. Some fell on rocky places, where it did not have much soil. It sprang up quickly, because the soil was shallow. But when the sun came up, the plants were scorched, and they withered because they had no root. Other seed fell among thorns, which grew up and choked the plants. Still other seed fell on good soil, where it produced a crop—a hundred, sixty or thirty times what was sown" (verses 3–8).

At its most basic level, this is a parable about faith because the farmer has faith in the seed, in its ability to yield a crop. In essence he's planting a seed of faith. If we're going to live lives that outlast us, then we must continually plant seeds of faith. While the parable focuses on God, who is always sowing faith into our lives, we're also invited to consider what we're planting, especially if we're going to live a life that produces for generations to come.

Every day, every moment, with every action, you're planting something. So the question is, what exactly are you planting? What is the cumulative effect of your words, actions, and intentions on those around you and those ahead of you? What harvest will be reaped from all that you plant day in and day out? From the outside, it may be difficult to discern between a seed and a pebble. But, of course, inside they're vastly different. There is life in the seed; there is nothing but rock inside the pebble. The seed has power and potential in it; it produces life. Unfortunately, some of us spend our time planting rocks—no potential, no life, no fruit.

When people look at your life from the outside, they may be impressed because you're planting "big things": a hefty bank account, major achievements, lofty goals, a weighty reputation. From all appearances, you're a successful farmer, but what fruit will these "big things" yield? It doesn't matter how significant your portfolio is or how ambitious your plans are. If all you're doing is accumulating things and trying to impress people, then the moment you die, your influence ends. The size of the rock doesn't matter. Whether it's a pebble or a boulder, if you plant it in the ground, it will never be seen again. Zero impact.

The crucial test in determining if we're planting real seeds or just rocks emerges in our motivation for planting. Am I sowing seed to meet my own needs or to meet the needs of others? In John 12:24, Jesus explains, "I tell you the truth, unless a kernel of wheat falls to the ground and dies, it remains only a single seed. But if it dies, it produces many seeds." The seed has to go into the ground, and in the silence of the ground, it dies. All alone there, it opens up to bring forth life. In the same way, we have to die to ourselves—to our selfish desires and goals and dreams—so we can plant an unselfish seed. People are created in God's image as spiritual beings who will live for eternity, either with Him or apart from Him. If we invest in people's lives, then our legacy becomes like a giant oak, providing life for generations to come.

Make It Count Moment

What did you do this last week that will last for the rest of this year? for ten years? for eternity? How much time did you spend this week reading God's Word compared to the time you spent reading the newspaper or watching television?

Soil Samples

Most farmers will tell you that *where* you plant is almost as important as *what* you plant. A seed has potential, but if it's planted in bad soil, there's not going to be any fruit. The soil in Jesus' parable represents different types of lives, and the first one represents a callous life. Jesus describes it this way: "When anyone hears the message about the kingdom and does not understand it, the evil one comes and snatches away what was sown in his heart. This is the seed sown along the path" (Matthew 13:19). This is the picture of people who are not interested in spiritual things at all. They're just living for themselves, planting selfish seeds. The impact of their lives will be like a footprint on the beach—here today and gone tomorrow.

The next type of soil represents a comfortable life. This is the picture of people who have committed their lives to following Jesus but are not growing deep in their relationship with Him. When problems and stresses set in, they give up. "The one who received the seed that fell on rocky places is the man who hears the word and at once receives it with joy. But since he has no root, he lasts only a short time. When trouble or persecution comes because of the word, he quickly falls away" (13:20–21). These people think that when they become a Christian, their lives will always go smoothly. But the Christian life is not about comfort; it's about character. God grows our character when we step out and plant seeds of faith, and it usually stretches us and makes us feel uncomfortable. In fact, "without faith it is impossible to please God" (Hebrews 11:6). God never promised a life that's convenient and carefree. He *does* promise us an abundant life of joy without worry if we'll look to Him daily for our needs. When we trust Him, life is a daring adventure where we step out in faith and become fully alive. He is a great God who wants to do amazing things in our lives.

Yet other seeds fall on a type of soil that represents the crowded life. This likely describes most of us. This seed begins to grow, but then the thorns and the weeds run rampant, and the young plant is choked out. "The one who received the seed that fell among the thorns is the man who hears the word, but the worries of this life and the deceitfulness of wealth choke it, making it unfruitful" (Matthew 13:22). This is the picture of people who start to follow God but surround themselves with things that won't last and can't produce life. Their days become completely crowded with too many items—many of them good things—that compete with what they know to be true. Soon the busyness chokes out time for their relationship with God. Just as in any relationship, the more time we spend with God, the better we'll know Him.

The final type of soil is the rich, fertile ground of the complete life that Jesus describes: "But the one who received the seed that fell on good soil is the man who hears the word and understands it. He produces a crop, yielding a hundred, sixty or thirty times what was sown" (13:23). This is a picture of people who receive God's truth, plant it deeply in their lives, and yield an impact that's felt for generations. That's what God wants to do in your life, but you must never lose sight of your fundamental motives: Why are you planting? What's your purpose or goal in life? "Do not be deceived: God cannot be mocked. A man reaps what he sows" (Galatians 6:7).

If you plant temporary things, you are going to harvest temporary things. If you plant eternal seeds, you are going to harvest eternal fruit. If you plant generosity, you are going to harvest generosity. If you give grace and compassion, you are going to get grace and compassion. Whatever you give out in life, you are going to get back. According to the law of the harvest, we reap *what* we sow, but we also reap much *more* than we sow. If I plant one seed, I don't get one seed or even one apple in return but a tree full of apples, season after season. A bushel of blessing comes from a tiny seed of faith.

If you want to know that your life matters, then you must be willing to plant eternal seeds in the fertile places of your life. When you focus on knowing God's Word and commit to loving others selflessly, you can expect a bumper crop of blessings in your life. Like the enveloping presence of a mighty oak, you will shelter future generations with the power of your timeless legacy.

Make It Last for Life

1. How much time do you spend reading, studying, and enjoying God's Word? How much time would you like to spend in the Word each week? Carve out some time in your schedule in the coming days and spend it alone with your Bible, knowing that this seed will produce fruit even after your life on this earth is over.

2. Make a list of your nonessential commitments, responsibilities, and
   obligations that may be worthwhile but will not last for eternity.
   Think about ways to transition these items out of your schedule, if
   not permanently, then at least for a season.

3. More important than our possessions are our values. Write down the
   values you hope to leave behind and who you hope will inherit them
   from you.

Sticks and Stones

USING ETERNAL BUILDING MATERIALS

> The price of anything
> is the amount of life you exchange for it.
> —HENRY DAVID THOREAU

> He is no fool who gives what he cannot keep
> to gain that which he cannot lose.
> —JIM ELLIOT

Shortly after the tsunami tragedy of 2004, I had the opportunity to visit the hardest-hit area of Indonesia: Banda Aceh. Despite my study and briefings for the trip, I was totally unprepared for the impact of experiencing the devastation firsthand. After traveling for many muddy miles, I came upon a bridge that is seared into my memory. It was a huge steel-and-concrete bridge that was once connected to a village of thousands of people. It now ended abruptly, dismembered midway by an impossibly big wave. I stood at the end and gazed down. Ocean. The entire village had been erased by the tsunami. I was standing on a bridge to nowhere.

The enormity of the loss represented by the gentle waves beneath me literally took my breath away. Then another thought hit me. We're all building bridges with our lives, but where are they leading? All our possessions on this earth will be washed away someday, but we last forever—we're eternal beings. One of our core desires is to leave this earth a better place than when we entered it. We're designed by our Creator to fulfill a vital purpose that no one else can accomplish but us. We're hard-wired with the longing to have an impact, to make a difference that will echo throughout eternity long after our bodies have turned to dust. Our legacy is like a bridge; obviously we'd like it not only to endure but to lead others to a significant destination in their lives. So much in this world feels temporary, fragile, finite. When entire villages can be wiped out in a matter of minutes and twin towers can be leveled within hours, it's difficult to believe that anything we do will have a lasting effect.

On a much smaller scale, most of us experience this on a daily basis, in the repetition of our schedules and mundane household duties. Parents of young children feel this keenly. We do the dishes, but after the next meal, the dishes are dirty again. We make up the beds in the morning, but by that night they're being slept in again. We cook a meal, but within a few hours or a few minutes, the kids are hungry again. We mop the sticky stuff off the floor, but before you know it, there's another spill. We pick up the kids from their lessons or their practices, but the next day we're taking them back. Recently my teenage daughter, Megan, ran the house for a full day while I was away. When I got home late that evening, my normally exuberant child was exhausted. I asked how her day had gone, and she said, "All day long I washed and folded clothes, made meals, did dishes, and cleaned the house...and *no one noticed*. I felt just like you!" It can be hard to feel like we're building a bridge to eternity when our accomplishments don't seem to last more than a day.

Make It Count Moment

What daily chores, routines, or responsibilities seem ceaseless in your life? Dishes? Cooking? E-mails? Phone calls? Driving? Ask God to help you remember that every little thing you do is noticed by Him.

Fire Drill
All of us desire to leave a legacy, to know that we mattered. And our legacy is determined by how we spend our days. As we've seen, the question becomes, will

our influence last beyond our lifetime? Paul was well aware of the correlation between the building materials we use and the quality of the construction. In 1 Corinthians 3:12–14 he wrote, "If any man builds on this foundation [Jesus Christ] using gold, silver, costly stones, wood, hay or straw, his work will be shown for what it is, because the Day will bring it to light. It will be revealed with fire, and the fire will test the quality of each man's work. If what he has built survives, he will receive his reward." Every day we get to choose the materials— either temporary or eternal—we'll build our lives with. If you want to ensure a legacy that will outlast you, that can withstand the ultimate fire drill, you need three key building materials.

The first one is your convictions—what you stand for. Convictions are those core values from God's Word that never change; they're eternal. Trends and styles—they come and go, "but the word of our God stands forever" (Isaiah 40:8). You only have to glance at the news occasionally to see that even so-called scientific studies can fluctuate or differ dramatically in interpretation. This week coffee is good for you. Next week it contributes to hypertension. This week protein diets do more harm than good; next month they're all the rage. Pop psychology, fashion trends, the bestseller list—they all come and go, up and down, round and round. But God's Word is solid and secure, without shifting in the slightest. It was the truth a thousand years ago, it's the truth today, and it will remain the truth a thousand years from now.

If we are to build an eternal legacy, our convictions have to come from God's Word. If your core values come from God's Word, they will never change. They are rock solid in a shaky world. The key to their effectiveness, however, is that we live them out. We must display congruence between what we believe and how we live. I like the way *The Message* puts this: "But if you just use my words in Bible studies and don't work them into your life, you are like a stupid carpenter who built his house on the sandy beach" (Matthew 7:26).

Studying the Bible isn't enough; we have to put it into our lives for it to be a conviction. You don't really believe something unless you live it out. There is a critical difference between beliefs and convictions: a belief is something you hold on to, but a conviction is something that holds you. A conviction is a core value from God's Word that anchors us, shapes us, permeates our lives, and becomes such a part of us that it's who we are.

Character Study

The next eternal building material emerges in our character. When we die, we don't take anything with us except our character, who we are at our core. From the very beginning, God has always had a plan, and it's to make you and me more like Jesus Christ, His Son. His plan is to put into our lives the very character traits of Christ. "God knew what he was doing from the very beginning. He decided from the outset to shape the lives of those who love him along the same lines as the life of his Son" (Romans 8:29, MSG).

Have you ever watched a master sculptor work? Sculptors have a vision for what's inside the marble or rock that they work toward revealing, little by little. I've been told that when the great sculptor Michelangelo was asked how he created his masterpiece *David*, he replied that he just chipped away everything that didn't look like David. Simple as that. And that's what God does in your life. He chips away everything in your character that doesn't look like Jesus Christ—all the character faults and flaws—because His plan is to perfect you in the image of His Son.

There are several methods God uses to cultivate Christ's character in us. The first comes with the problems of life. As difficult as they are, problems always have a purpose. Sometimes God allows distractions in your life, those little irritations that rub off the rough edges of your character. Other times He gets out the jackhammer and starts chipping away those huge chunks that don't look like Jesus. If we embrace the problems of life as opportunities to trust Him and become more like Christ, then we don't have nearly as much room to worry, feel sorry for ourselves, or get angry.

God also uses the pressures of life to smooth our edges. We learn patience under pressure. The most Christlike people I've ever known were experiencing tremendous stress and responsibility. Situations where we're squeezed always bring out what's inside us, be it bad or good. We can acknowledge our limitations and invite God to work in our lives, or we can get in the way and insist on doing things our way, even as our efforts crumble around us.

Finally, He likes to use the people in our lives to enrich our character, to chip away at our selfish edges that prevent us from loving others the way Christ does. Every one of us has people in our lives who are hard to love. Just because we love someone doesn't mean that the relationship will go smoothly. Remember that God is using people as His chisel to chip away everything in your life that doesn't look like Christ so He can make your life a work of art.

Make It Count Moment

In what area of your life are you currently experiencing the most pressure? How have you responded to it so far? How might God be using it to build your character?

Bridge Building

Eternal legacies are built on our convictions, our character, and our community. Godly convictions and godly character last forever, and our relationships with God's people last forever as well. If we are to forge a bridge that leads to an eternal destination, then we need teammates—people committed to the same passion for God and His Word. Otherwise, we're building bridges that trail off in midair when our bodies die and we leave this earth.

If you're too busy to commit to ongoing time with a group of like-minded individuals, then you're just too busy. You may remember the sisters Mary and Martha, who were friends of Jesus. One night they invited Him over for dinner, and Martha was running around in a frenzy trying to make sure everything was perfect because the Son of God was in her house. But Mary just sat at Jesus' feet listening to Him, relaxing and enjoying some quality time. Needless to say, Martha was pretty ticked about the whole situation. She was mad at Mary, and I think she was really mad at Jesus because He wasn't setting her sister straight: "Martha was distracted by all the preparations that had to be made. She came to him and asked, 'Lord, don't you care that my sister has left me to do the work by myself? Tell her to help me!' 'Martha, Martha,' the Lord answered, 'you are worried and upset about many things, but only one thing is needed. Mary has chosen what is better'" (Luke 10:40–42).

Jesus has this way of tender-heartedly driving the knife of truth into our hearts and twisting right where we need it. His words must have hurt poor Martha. She was thinking, *Lord, do You see all I'm doing? I'm working as hard as I can, and look what You're letting Mary do. You know, You're God's Son. Why don't You tell her to help me?* Jesus kindly told her, "My friend, you're missing the boat. Your priorities are all wrong, Martha. Mary is doing the thing that's most important and that will last, the only thing that's eternal. You're making the Christian life too complicated! It's really pretty simple. All that really matters is a relationship with Me and a relationship with others."

If we only expected to live a few weeks, the choice to focus on Jesus and on those around us would be clearer and easier. As we've seen in numerous ways, building an eternal legacy requires investing in other people. The often-overlooked reality is that at least some of those people must share our goals. They may not be going about it the same way we would (just as Mary didn't help prepare the meal the way Martha wanted her to), but if they're pursuing God and we know their hearts, then we can trust that we share a common bond.

Most of the material possessions we'll leave behind won't last much longer than we did. Our money will be spent, our homes and property will deteriorate or be sold, our personal belongings will become items in an antique store. I recently saw an antique store called Dead People's Stuff. That's funny, but it's an honest description of what all our possessions will someday be. But if we build our lives on convictions, character, and community, then we will have established an eternal memorial that will benefit countless lives for untold generations. We will have spent our lives creating a bridge that ultimately leads others to God, and there's no more satisfying legacy than that.

Make It Last for Life

1. Grab some paper and a pen, and number from one to five. List five convictions that you hold and believe are timeless. Go back over each one and reflect on its basis. How is it reinforced by God's Word? by the lives of others? by your own experience?

2. Number from one to five again, this time listing character traits you would like to be remembered for after you've left this earth. How

have you seen God cultivate these in your life? Which ones does He seem to be concentrating on right now?

3. Finally, make one more list from one to five. Write down the names of five people—not family and not co-workers—who share your convictions and commitment to godly character. How often do you see each one? How could you encourage them? In what areas could they hold you more accountable? Consider doing the *One Month to Live* small-group Bible study together. Go to www.OneMonthTo Live.com for more information.

Collisions

STAYING THE COURSE WHEN YOUR LIFE CRASHES

> Happiness is not a goal; it is a by-product.
> —ELEANOR ROOSEVELT

> When you were born, you were crying,
> and everyone around you was smiling.
> Live your life so that when you die, you will be smiling,
> and everyone around you will be crying.
> —ANONYMOUS

*W*hen I was a kid, one of my favorite toys was the SST Smash 'Em Up Derby Cars. They came with these big flywheels in the middle and a rip cord. You'd pull the rip cord and aim the cars at each other, and there would be this massive collision. Parts would fly everywhere. It was a glorious thing!

The Smash 'Em Up Derby Cars were designed so you could easily put the parts back on and quickly have another demolition derby. I still remember the jingle that was in the commercial: "Smash, bang, crash 'em up, put 'em back again. SST Smash 'Em Up Derby. Batteries not required." It was just so cool as a kid to create a huge collision and then be able to put all the pieces back together again, no damage done.

I wish life were that way. But it's not so easy to put the pieces back together when life's crashes occur. Sometimes our lives get off track, and we get on a collision course and don't know how to apply the brakes. It usually starts with what we think is a time crunch. Our schedule gets overloaded, we feel overwhelmed, the walls start closing in, everything starts to collide, and we realize we just don't have enough time to get it all done.

We usually think we have a time-management problem and hope that buying a new electronic gadget will solve it. But time management is just the surface issue. If we only had one month to live, we would likely adjust our calendars and drill down to the deeper causes of our discomfort. We would discover a couple of basic causes of most of life's collisions. If we want to leave an enduring legacy, we have to get on the right road with the Master Driver.

Make It Count Moment

When was the last time you experienced a life collision, a season or experience in which you found yourself coming apart at the seams? How did you respond to it? How will you respond to the next collision differently based on what you learned from that experience?

Crash Course

The first cause is a collision of values. What we perceive as schedule-related collisions are usually values-based crashes. Our actions reveal a different set of values than what we say matters most to us. For example, we say our health is important, but sometimes we don't eat right or exercise. Or maybe you say your family is your main priority, but work often takes precedence over time with them. You may say that God is number one in your priorities, but the reality is that He gets your leftovers in time, talent, and finances. One of the greatest sources of stress and frustration in our lives is this collision of values. If our time was suddenly limited to a short period on this earth, we would finally work hard to align our actions with our beliefs.

The good news is that we can examine our lives and look for these collision points and change the track we're on. We can begin to realign our priorities with our performance right now. The best way to begin this process is to examine a more serious collision: a collision of wills. Sometimes my will collides with God's will. Consider how this applies to time management. God created me. He also created a day to contain twenty-four hours. So if I can't get everything done that I need to do within that twenty-four-hour period, then I'm focusing on some things God never intended for me to do. At the risk of overgeneralizing, I assert it's as simple as that. God has given us enough time to get done everything He wants us to do. If we rest in this knowledge and trust Him for what must be accomplished each day, our inner striving fades as we rely more on His plans.

We get to choose which path we take in life. We can travel in God's direction, or we can chart our own course and try to make it on our own. We can drive the car empowered by His will or the one fueled by our will. When I choose to drive my own car and make all my decisions without consulting Him, it's like heading the wrong way down a one-way street. It ends in a collision with God, which isn't pretty. Only when we allow Him to direct us can we leave a lasting impact. "Trust in the LORD with all your heart and lean not on your own understanding; in all your ways acknowledge him, and he will make your paths straight" (Proverbs 3:5–6).

Make It Count Moment

On a scale of one to ten, with one being totally following your will and ten being totally following God's will, where are you presently? In what areas of your life do you see the greatest discrepancy between your will and His—relationships, finances, spiritual growth, something else?

Willpower

So how do we stay in the middle of God's will? The Psalmist instructs us: "Trust in the LORD and do good; dwell in the land and enjoy safe pasture. Delight yourself in the LORD and he will give you the desires of your heart. Commit your way to the LORD; trust in him and he will do this" (Psalm 37:3–5).

How do we avoid those nasty collisions where our will gets in the way of His perfect plan for our lives? If we break down this passage and dig deep, we're going to find three principles for staying in God's will. The first one is really an issue of trust: "Trust in the LORD and do good." If we trust God, then we'll want to obey

Him rather than follow our own desires. If we don't trust Him, we'll want to get behind the steering wheel and take control.

This principle reminds me of a recent experience with my two older sons. They're both good drivers, but when they first started, I have to admit I wasn't very good at sitting in the passenger's seat. I would hold on and grit my teeth and try not to say too much. I soon discovered that I really couldn't criticize them for things they had learned from riding with me over the years. Teenagers don't let you get away with anything; they have an incredibly high hypocrisy meter! My sons would go 40 in a 35-mph zone, and I'd say, "You have to go the speed limit. Police patrol this area regularly. You're going to get a ticket." Once my son Ryan looked at me and said, "I never see you drive 35 on this street." Ouch.

After one such driving lesson, one son literally looked over at me and said, "You've got a control problem." He nailed me. I do have a control issue, and it's especially acute when it comes to God's will. So do you. It's really not so much about God's will as it is about God's wheel. It's really a struggle over control of the steering wheel.

We're always trying to wrestle the steering wheel away from God. We think we can drive better than He does. We're always telling Him how to drive and where to go, thinking, *I know what's best for my life.* Oh, we let God drive as long as it's along the route that we would have chosen. But when we can't figure out what He's up to, we get nervous. So often, since we can't see where He's going or how we'll get there, we freak out and grab the wheel again. This is when we have to learn to relax and relinquish control of the wheel to the Master Driver. We have to learn to trust Him enough to say, "I don't know what to do here, but I want what You want more than anything else. I want Your will. Keep me from making a mistake." When we get to this place, then God directs our paths and aligns us with His purposes for our lives.

But there is another principle to staying in God's will. Not only do I need to trust, but I also need to delight. The Psalmist says, "Delight yourself in the LORD and he will give you the desires of your heart" (verse 4). This word "delight" in Hebrew means "to enjoy." When you delight in someone, you enjoy their company, and you want to spend time with them. We all want to receive the fulfillment of our heart's desires, and this scripture makes it clear that this is possible. But there's a condition—it's a promise with a premise. We must delight ourselves in the Lord *more* than we long for our heart's desires. This is where many people seem to lose sight of what God's will is all about. We think He should let us drive the car if He really loves us. But He wants us to long to be with Him, to know Him, to love Him more than any destination we could ever reach on our own.

When our oldest son first got his driver's license, he couldn't wait to get out of the house and be independent. There was always a ball game, a study session, an event—something that required him to drive somewhere. But then one Friday night I was surprised to see him sitting at the dinner table with the rest of the family. I commented, "I'm glad to see you, but what are you doing here?" He smiled and quietly said, "I just wanted to hang at home tonight. Missed you guys." Wow. That made my day! God is the same way. He longs for us to delight in Him more than we delight in our own freedom. In fact, when we delight in Him, our heart's desires often change. We no longer want our way; we want His way.

Finally, if we're going to remain in the center of God's will, we must trust, delight, and commit. "Commit your way to the LORD; trust in him and he will do this" (verse 5). We have to come to the place where we commit to following God's will. Often we say, "God, show me Your will, and I'll consider it as an option in this decision I'm making." God says, "No, you have to commit to following My will, and *then* I'll show you what it is."

Maybe you feel like your life has crashed and the pieces are crumpled beyond recognition or repair. It seems you're the object of a lot of rubbernecking—a messed-up life that others stare at. I have news for you. It's not too late to change the course of your life! God still has a great plan for you, but the first step is to slide out of the driver's seat and ask God to take the wheel. Start giving Him the first consideration in every decision, and watch your life be transformed.

Which brings us back to trust. Obedience starts with trust and ends with trust. We step out in faith and allow God to drive our car and take us where He wants us to be. But it's not a passive process. He wants us to pay attention and take action along the way. Most of an enduring legacy results from actions we take in our lifetime. We say we want to be close to our loved ones, but this can only be accomplished through quality and quantity time, honest conversations, and shared sorrows and celebrations. We say we want to make a difference in this world, to leave it a better place than we found it. But we must take action, directed by our Father, to reach out to others, loving them, mentoring them, serving them.

Our time in this life is limited. If we truly want to ensure that we've fulfilled our purpose when it's our time to go, then we must stay squarely in God's will, trusting, delighting, and committing to His path. He's the only One who can rebuild our lives and redirect us when our will collides with His.

Make It Last for Life

1. What's the greatest barrier to trusting God in your life right now? What past experiences have left you doubtful, angry, hurt, or disappointed? Spend some time in prayer, either writing or talking to God about these experiences. It can be difficult to build trust with Him if you're not communicating.

2. Make a list from one to five, and write down the desires of your heart. Be as honest with yourself as possible. Spend some time reflecting on each desire and why you long for it. Commit your list to God, asking for His perspective regarding each item.

3. If you only had one month to live, what three actions would you want to take to align your remaining time with God's will? What's keeping you from pursuing them now? Choose one, and begin to implement it this week.

Starfish

MAKING A WORLD OF DIFFERENCE

> The true measure of an individual is how he treats a person
> who can do him absolutely no good.
> —ANN LANDERS

> The only thing necessary for the triumph of evil
> is for good men to do nothing.
> —EDMUND BURKE

*L*ife has definitely changed a lot since I was a kid. When it comes to our children, we're a lot more safety conscious than our parents were. People in my generation actually rode bikes with no helmets and rode in cars with no air bags. We even drank water straight out of the garden hose and lived to tell about it! There's nothing wrong with being protective of our children—my kids accuse me of being overprotective all the time. The problem comes when we start thinking happiness means being safe and comfortable and when our goal in life becomes the avoidance of all risk. When our top priority is to be safe and secure, we lose touch not just with the needs of others but with a primary need of our own.

We were created for so much more than punching buttons and scrolling screens. We were created for a grand adventure! God designed us to take great risks and face huge challenges, to accomplish mighty goals that will have a lasting impact.

If you discovered that you only had one month to live and you began considering how you could leave a lasting global legacy, you might be tempted to think, *It's too late. I don't have the money or power needed to make a difference in this world.* But never underestimate the power of *one.* It's the ability each of us has, every day, to be used by God to bless the rest of the world.

Make It Count Moment

How important is comfort to you at this stage of your life? What conveniences would be the hardest for you to give up? Your computer? Microwave? iPod? Mattress? Coffee maker?

Power of One

A businessman visiting a resort community left his hotel early one morning to take a walk. When he reached the shoreline, he came upon a stunning sight: countless starfish had washed up on the beach during the night in a high tide. They were still moving, still alive, clambering all over one another, trying to get back into the ocean. He knew it wouldn't be long until the tropical sun would bake the poor creatures trapped there on the sand. He wished he could do something, but there were thousands of them, as far as his eye could see, and there was no way he could make a dent in saving them.

So he went on his way. Walking farther down the beach, he came upon a little boy who leaned over, scooped up a starfish, and flung it like a Frisbee into the ocean. He repeated the process over and over again, picking up speed, obviously trying to save as many as possible.

Once the man realized what the little boy was doing, he felt it was his responsibility to help the boy by informing him of a harsh life lesson. He walked up to the child and said, "Son, let me tell you. What you're doing here is noble, but you can't save all these starfish. There are thousands of them. The sun's getting really hot, and they're all going to die. You might as well just go on your way and play. You really can't make a difference here."

The little boy didn't say anything at first; he just stared at the businessman.

Then he stooped down and picked up another starfish, flung it out into the ocean as far as he could, and said, "Well, I just made *all* the difference for that one."

Often children have more to teach us than we have to teach them—certainly in this case. This boy did not allow the magnitude of the situation to keep him from doing what he could do: save one starfish at a time. Perhaps Helen Keller summed it up best: "I am only one, but still I am one. I cannot do everything, but still I can do something; and because I cannot do everything, I will not refuse to do something that I can do."

When we are reminded on the nightly newscast of global problems like world hunger, the AIDS epidemic, war, and famine, we often respond with numbing apathy or resigned defeat. Most of us are tempted to think, *Why even try? The issue is so enormous and complex that I'll never make a difference.* There is a temptation to make these problems abstractions instead of daily realities for individual human lives. But if we realign our view with God's perspective and take it one starfish at a time, we will do what we can do, no matter how small or inconsequential our efforts may appear. If we touch one life, we may make the difference between life and death—physical as well as spiritual—for another human being. If we make it a habit to do what we can, when we can, where we can, we will be transformed as we help others. As Ralph Waldo Emerson observed, "There is no beautifier of complexion, or form, or behavior, like the wish to scatter joy and not pain around us."

Living Sacrifice

We rarely face it, but many of us have a nagging question in the depths of our soul. How do we reconcile the fact that we're living in nice homes, driving nice cars, and eating plenty of food while most of the world lives on less than two dollars a day? You read correctly. Three billion people in our world right now live on less than the U.S. equivalent of two dollars a day. As we drive our kids to soccer practice in our SUVs, how do we reconcile our lifestyle with the fact that kids in San José, Costa Rica, or Nairobi, Kenya, or thousands of other cities around the world play soccer on streets filled with raw sewage and kick balls made from trash and duct tape?

I'm not trying to make you feel guilty, only to remind you that we have lost our perspective. We've lost our ability to see beyond our own lives for two primary reasons. One is the human desire to control our own safe and comfortable world. The other is that our culture drives us to acquire more rather than give away more.

If we knew our time on earth was running out, we'd want to do all we could to impact others. We wouldn't want the regret of a life misspent and self-absorbed. We would want to know that we honored the God we love by being the very best stewards of all He has given us. In his letter to the Romans, Paul wrote, "Therefore, I urge you, brothers, in view of God's mercy, to offer your bodies as living sacrifices, holy and pleasing to God—this is your spiritual act of worship. Do not conform any longer to the pattern of this world, but be transformed by the renewing of your mind. Then you will be able to test and approve what God's will is—his good, pleasing and perfect will" (12:1–2).

Is it okay to drink our daily lattes? to have nice things? to enjoy the blessings in our lives? Yes. But if we long for something substantial to leave behind, then we have to wake up and realize that our maturity fuels the fulfillment of this goal. Paul reveals the secret to maturity: we must move from our focus on self-comfort and become living sacrifices. The goal of maturity is to move beyond ourselves and our own desires. If we truly want to grow in our character and our faith, then we must be willing to change our goal from one of safety to one of sacrifice.

One of the first and most important ways we can begin to care more about others is to pray for the poor and oppressed throughout the world. Pray for their needs. For their healing. For religious and political freedom. For food and clean water and vital medicine. When we start praying for the hurting people on the other side of the world, we begin caring about them, and we want to learn more about the details of their lives. It connects our hearts to theirs. We're more mindful of what we have, how we can use it, and why we've been entrusted with it. Yes, God already knows the needs of everyone throughout the world. But prayer focuses you and me on the needs of others in a unique way. We're forced to look beyond ourselves and to rely on God to show us how to love and help those we're praying for.

Make It Count Moment

How often do you let opportunities pass you by because your contribution feels too small? What are the "starfish" situations in your life? Do you tend to respond more like the boy or the businessman? Why?

Action Required

Often we're inspired to love others by giving of ourselves—offering what we have to help them overcome their problems and enrich their lives. We offer our bodies as living sacrifices when we give of our time, our talent, and our treasure. If you want to experience the full adventure that your life is intended to be, then you have to be willing to take action and serve those in need with God's love. The Bible has a lot to say about caring for the needs of the poor. "If a man shuts his ears to the cry of the poor, he too will cry out and not be answered" (Proverbs 21:13). God holds us accountable for how we use our blessings to help the poor and hurting.

Our greatest gifts—time, talents, and treasures—are essential to this process of maturing and building a global legacy. We've already discussed the value of time as our most precious and limited commodity. If you want to sacrifice something that no one else can give, then give part of your time to someone else. No one controls this commodity but you. How you spend your time reveals what's planted most firmly in your heart.

As far as talents go, we all have talents, every single one of us. But we devise all kinds of excuses: "Well, I'm really not a Bible scholar, so I can't teach or do missions" or "I really don't have much money left over to support charity." But think about what you can do. Consider the expertise you have in the jobs you've worked—whether it's construction, banking, sales, medicine, or education. You have knowledge, abilities, and skills that can change the lives of others if you'll only share them. Can you listen and care? offer a smile? hug a child? Most of us underestimate the power we have just by being present in the life of someone else.

Money and how we spend it also reveal a great deal about who we are and what we value. God says it's okay to be blessed financially as long as we do two things with our money and possessions. Number one: enjoy what we have instead of always wanting more. And number two: give generously. If we do these two things, we'll grow in maturity and enjoy a level of satisfaction that money can never buy. But if we hoard our blessings and take God's goodness for granted, our hearts will harden, and we'll never be able to reconcile with the things that matter most.

The final way we grow in maturity and create a world-conscious heart is to work in community. Whether it's through our churches, our schools, our companies, our neighborhoods, or our families, we're called to come together to help others. "For just as you have many members in one physical body and those members differ in their functions, so we, though many in number, compose one body in Christ and are all members of one another. Through the grace of God we have different gifts" (Romans 12:4–6, Phillips). Together we can literally change the world.

Make It Last for Life

1. For the next month, choose one item of comfort, luxury, or convenience that you'll do without. It might be your daily Starbucks, the half-hour sitcom before bed, your favorite dessert, or something similar. Use the time or money that generally goes to this item for a larger purpose—praying, contributing to world philanthropy or missions, or offering your services to someone in need. Similar to the practice of giving up something for the season of Lent before Easter, this exercise can help you regain perspective on what it means to be a living sacrifice.

2. What cause, situation, or people group have you always been moved by? It might be the war-torn Middle East, people with AIDS in your own city, or missions in China, but most of us have been drawn at one time or another to a concern outside our usual orbit. This week spend some time praying for these people and researching ways you can serve them—using your time, your talents, and your treasure. Commit to a specific goal that will meet some of the needs of the people facing these issues. Log on to www.OneMonthToLive.com to see how you can unite with a community of people to make a huge difference.

3. Needs are all around us, and we don't have to leave our neighborhood, let alone our country, to give sacrificially. This week initiate a local service project in your area. You might work with your church, a

community Web site (blog sites are great for this), or your department at work. Commit to a specific goal—for instance, making home repairs for a single mom or widow, collecting clothes for a shelter, or raising money for relief funds. Set a date, and determine the role each person in the group will play in meeting the need and getting the job done.

Footprint

LEAVING A LASTING IMPRESSION

> My children will not remember the words of wisdom
> I've passed along over the years,
> nor will yours remember the good advice you've given.
> However, etched in their minds and planted in their hearts
> is a permanent picture of who you are
> and how you've lived before them.
> —DOROTHY KELLEY PATTERSON

> We make a living by what we get;
> we make a life by what we give.
> —WINSTON CHURCHILL

*A*wareness of what it means to "go green" continues to gain momentum. It seems like more and more people today are concerned with their ecological footprint. As global warming, recycling, reliance on fossil fuels, and pollution remain significant issues, we should strive to leave as small an environmental footprint as possible. We want to be good stewards of our planet because of the responsibility that God has entrusted to us regarding His creation. But while we look for ways to decrease our environmental footprint, we should seek to increase our spiritual footprint. We need to make the most positive, the most lasting imprint on people's lives possible. To do that, we have to get incredibly intentional about the kind of impression we're making on other people's lives.

Many times our spiritual priorities converge with practical application. I'll never forget a recent campaign at our church when we learned about a shortage of shoes at our Houston homeless shelters. Many people had contributed blankets and food, but few realized how desperately the homeless need warm, sturdy shoes. So at the end of a service, I shared my vision that we could make a huge difference in just one weekend, and I asked all who felt so led to take off their shoes and leave them up front and then walk out in their socks or bare feet and feel the pavement many homeless men and women experience every day. The church overwhelmingly rose to the challenge. We collected over forty-five hundred pairs of shoes that day and solved the shoe problem in Houston for many months to come.

This is the kind of impact we can work toward every day. We don't have to become foreign missionaries, be ultrarich, or quit our day jobs. If we want to impact those who follow us, we simply have to love God, serve others, and give from what we've been given. One of the best ways we can contribute to our unique spiritual footprint is by the way we treat others.

Make It Count Moment

Think of a recent experience when your spiritual beliefs led to a practical application of serving others. What need in others did the experience meet? What need in you did it meet?

Pollution Solution

Just as we must control our emissions of toxic industrial gases and curb pollution, we must also deal with the clutter that accumulates in our souls. It can be tempting to overlook our own faults and shortcomings and focus exclusively on the mistakes of those around us. We've all met people who pride themselves on their spirituality and point out everyone else's faults while ignoring their own.

God calls us to look within and examine our own conscience without judging everyone else. Isaiah 1:18 says, "No matter how deep the stain of your sins, I can remove it. I can make you as clean as freshly fallen snow. Even if you are stained as red as crimson, I can make you as white as wool" (NLT). We've all made mistakes, chosen poorly, and hurt the ones we love most. We may try to cover up the garbage in our soul, ignore it, and pretend it's not there, but that doesn't take away the pollution eroding and choking our hearts. We judge others, comparing ourselves in ways that make us feel like we're better because we haven't committed the same mistakes. But sin is sin. You and I may have different sins in our lives, but they all keep us short of God's standard. Every one of us has experienced a polluted soul, because we've all sinned.

The life-transforming news is that Jesus Christ forgives and cleanses us of even the deepest debris. Most people who know they are approaching the end of their lives are forced to face their faults, regrets, and mistakes. They are often more eager to embrace the gift of God's grace than ever before. The good news is that we have this gift available to us every day, whether we have four weeks or many years left on this earth.

If we want to leave a legacy of grace for those who come after us, we must begin by acknowledging our personal need for God's forgiveness. One of the best ways to do this is by examining our conscience each day. When we keep short accounts with God, we prevent the spiritual debris from accumulating and blocking our ability to love and serve.

Make It Count Moment

How do you usually respond when you reflect on your sins and short-comings? Does it typically drive you to God's grace or deeper into hiding? How do you usually respond to the flaws and sins of others? What's the correlation between how you view your own sin and how you view the sin of others?

Recycling Grace

When people experience the forgiveness and love of God through the gift of His Son, they're often ready to ask for forgiveness from those they've wounded and to extend mercy to those who've hurt them. With the freedom and joy they experience as a result of God's forgiveness, they become empowered to face some of the hard chapters of their lives.

In fact, as Jesus explains in one of His parables, there's a reciprocal relationship between the forgiveness we experience and the forgiveness we extend. I like to think of it as recycling grace—giving generously what we've received from God. After an indebted servant begs his king for mercy for the great debt he owes, the same servant then has another servant imprisoned for his inability to repay him much less than he had owed the king. Such a double standard doesn't cut it in God's kingdom: "The king summoned the man and said, 'You evil servant! I forgave your entire debt when you begged me for mercy. Shouldn't you be compelled to be merciful to your fellow servant who asked for mercy?' The king was furious and put the screws to the man until he paid back his entire debt. And that's exactly what my Father in heaven is going to do to each one of you who doesn't forgive unconditionally anyone who asks for mercy" (Matthew 18:32–35, MSG).

If we judge others less and confess our own shortcomings more, then we will be investing in an eternal legacy—our character and its effect on future generations. Asking for forgiveness and admitting our hurts may never be as easy or as natural as we'd like it to be. But if we knew we might not have another opportunity to make our relationships right, we'd take every possible opportunity to convey our sorrow over how we had hurt others. Proverbs tells us that the person "who conceals his sins does not prosper, but whoever confesses and renounces them finds mercy" (28:13). Confessing the fullness of our hearts can restore a level of peace that our pride, anger, and self-righteousness rob us of.

Too often we try to make amends with others without really accepting and experiencing the power of grace in our lives. We think we have to try extra hard to make it up to those we've offended and to keep quiet about those who have hurt us, pretending that nothing happened. But when we encounter the radical power of God's grace, it's literally life changing.

God loves you just the way you are, but He loves you too much to let you stay that way. Philippians 2:13 puts it this way: "For God is working in you, giving you the desire to obey him and the power to do what pleases him" (NLT). Our Father empowers us to live transformed lives when we admit our mistakes and their consequences. The Bible says God gives grace to the humble, but He opposes the proud (Proverbs 3:34). So when we humble ourselves and say, "God, I need You to give me the power to change; I need You to give me the power to love; I need You to give me the power to do the things You ask me to do," then He fills us with His power and His strength.

Christ finds us in the middle of our mess, but He doesn't say, "Hey, clean up your act, and then I'll think about loving you." No, the Bible says that while I was still a sinner, Christ reached down and picked me up, and He held me close and forgave me. When one of my children was a potty-training preschooler, he had an accident in front of several adult friends of mine. As he realized what had happened, he reacted with embarrassment and shame. He looked up at me and said, "Hold me!" How did I respond? Did I say, "No way! Gross! Go clean yourself up, and *then* I'll hold you!" Of course not! I scooped him up and held him close because he's my son, and I love him, no matter what.

Grace accepts me where I am, but grace also gives me the power to change. Titus 2:11–12 says, "For the grace of God that brings salvation has appeared to all men. It teaches us to say 'No' to ungodliness and worldly passions, and to live self-controlled, upright and godly lives in this present age." When we're in the atmosphere of God's grace and feel totally accepted, we crave change. We want to know Him and be more like Him.

If you only had one month to live, you would almost certainly want to do some things differently in your life. The problem is that no lasting changes can be made unless we're transformed and energized by the ultimate power source, the grace of God. We can never hope to make a good exit from our lives without it. We can't leave a lasting spiritual footprint unless we walk a mile in the shoes of others, forgiving them just as we've been forgiven.

We're all trophies of grace. "Accept one another, then, just as Christ accepted you, in order to bring praise to God" (Romans 15:7). We're to accept each other and display the love of Christ to those around us. This can mean confronting others at times or humbling ourselves to confess and ask for their forgiveness. Only God's grace can allow us to let go of past hurts and forgive others. Only His grace can motivate us to set our pride, shame, guilt, and regret aside and ask others to forgive us. The more we can put the practice of grace into our lives, the greater the legacy we will leave. Author Jackie Windspear put it this way: "Grace isn't a little prayer you chant before receiving a meal. It's a way to live."

Make It Last for Life

1. Think of a loved one who has passed away. How would you describe his or her spiritual legacy? What would you like to emulate about this person's legacy of character? What would you like to avoid?

2. Spend some time with God in prayer and confession. Ask Him to reveal His grace to you in a new way, one that helps you better grasp the fullness of His love for you. Go to someone you've offended or hurt and ask for forgiveness.

3. Is there anyone who needs your forgiveness? Reflect on the high price God paid to forgive you, and then ask Him what action, if any, He wants you to take in relationship to that person.

Game Over

DYING TO LIVE

If I discover within myself a desire
which no experience in this world can satisfy,
the most probable explanation is
that I was made for another world.
—C. S. LEWIS

Never be afraid to trust an unknown future to a known God.
—CORRIE TEN BOOM

*Y*ou don't have to be a sports fan to appreciate the excitement, passion, and drama of two well-matched opponents on the field. Whether it's a tie game broken by the game-winning home run in the last inning of your child's Little League game or the last-second field goal made from fifty yards away to win the Super Bowl, we all love to witness those miraculous, come-from-behind wins.

When it comes to the game of life, though, there will come a moment when the final buzzer sounds, and it's game over. In fact, statistics show that the human death rate is at a constant 100 percent! You can't avoid it; you can't cheat your way around it. Eventually you will experience a moment at the end of life when the final buzzer will sound and no miraculous play will send you into overtime. When our bodies finally wear out, we exit the life we've known on earth. We're forced to enter the process of whatever happens next.

A recent poll shows that 81 percent of Americans believe in life after death. It used to be that nobody really wanted to talk about this subject, but more and more people are fascinated by those who have brushes with death or who think they have insight into what happens after we draw our final breaths. As I've emphasized throughout this book, embracing our mortality can liberate us to live as fully as possible. In Ecclesiastes, we're told, "A wise person thinks much about death, while the fool thinks only about having a good time now" (7:4, NLT). It's wise to approach life with an end in mind. It's foolish to ignore the inevitable. Thinking about what's going to happen when the final buzzer sounds brings a sharpness of focus to life. It helps us to live a more intentional life and to make every moment count.

Make It Count Moment

What reminders of your mortality have you encountered this week? An ache or a pain? Medication taken for a health condition? Your first gray hair? Something else? How do you usually feel when you face these little reminders?

Heaven Can't Wait

God put you on this earth for a reason, and He has a plan for your life. But this life is not the end. Scripture is very clear about this reality. One day you will stop breathing, but you won't stop living. You'll live forever in eternity.

One moment after you die, you'll experience either the greatest celebration ever or the greatest separation ever. Heaven and hell are real places, and we have the choice of where we will spend eternity. God could have created us as robots, programmed to love Him, serve Him, and follow Him. But He didn't do that. He took the greatest risk of all when He created us with this power called free will. God loves you so much that He died for you, but He lets you choose whether or not you will love Him back and desire to be with Him for all eternity.

We were designed to be in perfect relationship with God. We were created with a homesickness for the eternal reality of a place beyond our wildest dreams. As the old hymn explains, "This world is not my home." Heaven is our heart's home, where the homecoming party goes on and on and on. But it's also a place of "no more"—no more tears, grief, loss, or death. "He will wipe every tear from their eyes. There will be no more death or mourning or crying or pain, for the old order of things has passed away" (Revelation 21:4).

People have often thought of heaven as a mystical place where we'll sit on clouds. We're secretly afraid we'll get tired of this perfect place and be bored with the monotony of the halos and mist. But that wouldn't be heaven, would it? No, the Bible says heaven is a perfect place full of adventure and excitement.

The Bible talks about heaven and uses human words to describe what is humanly indescribable. It says there will be streets of gold and gates of pearls. The place drips with value and significance, meaning and purpose. We'll have jobs there that will bring us ultimate fulfillment. Christ is there, so we will experience more compassion and creativity than we could ever dream of. We'll have new, perfect bodies. We'll be reunited with our family, friends, and loved ones who are there. So much joy, peace, and splendor will converge for us that we can only imagine what it will be like.

If we want to experience heaven, then we must live each moment here on earth prepared for eternity. You're not really ready to live until you're ready to die. And you don't have to be worried about it. You can determine your destination right now if you haven't already. If you're not sure that you have eternal life right now, if you're not sure you'll be in heaven one day, then you can finish this chapter knowing for sure. "And this is what God has testified: He has given us eternal life, and this life is in his Son. So whoever has God's Son has life; whoever does not have his Son does not have life" (1 John 5:11–12, NLT). Basically, getting into heaven is all about who you know. If you know the Son, you get in. If you don't know the Son, you don't.

Heaven is a perfect place for perfect people, and the problem is, we're not perfect. We've all sinned. That's why Christ came to take our place—so we could join Him in heaven one day. Not that we could ever deserve it, not that we could ever earn it, but He has made the way for us. The Bible says that, because of what

Christ has done, we are friends with God. Right now you can pray and ask Christ to come into your life and forgive your past guilt and sins and give you a future in heaven one day. You don't have to be afraid of eternity. God loves you more than you can fathom. He truly does. You really can't make the most of every moment until you know your eternity is settled. That knowledge then frees you to enjoy life and to make a difference in others' lives.

Make It Count Moment

According to a recent poll, 74 percent of Americans believe in heaven and hell. Do you? How would you describe each of them to a friend or someone you love? What has shaped your descriptions of these two places—books, movies, television, Scripture, sermons, something else?

Eternal Assurance

Once you're prepared for eternity, you want to invest in what will last forever as well. Your perspective shifts. You begin to realize that much of what we value and focus on is insignificant and meaningless in light of eternity.

We often live as if we are going to be on this earth forever. Think of it this way. Let's say you went on vacation and checked into your hotel room, where you planned to stay for a couple of weeks. But you didn't like the appearance of the room, so you called in your own interior decorator. You put a lot of money into it and changed the wallpaper, the curtains, the artwork—the whole room. Then you wanted a bigger television, so you bought an oversized flat screen and had it mounted on the wall. When you went outside, you didn't like the shrubs and the flowers, so you hired a landscaper. You kept making changes to suit yourself. Then you went home.

That's exactly what many of us do today on this earth. We act as if we're going to be here forever. We concentrate on things that seem really important to us at the moment but that ultimately don't last. Our focus needs to be redirected to the things that will pass the test of time, and really there are only two: God's Word and people. The Bible says the grass withers and the flowers fade, but the Word of God stands forever (Isaiah 40:8). So when you spend time in God's Word—building your character, becoming more like Christ, learning the values from God's Word, and applying them—that lasts forever. You take that with you into eternity. The other eternal investment you can make is in people. People live forever in eternity. So anytime you make a difference in the lives of others, it will last forever. That's why relationships are the most important thing in your life.

Too often we focus on things that just don't last. Look at Ecclesiastes 11:7–8: "It is a wonderful thing to be alive! If a person lives to be very old, let him rejoice in every day of life, but let him also remember that eternity is far longer, and that everything down here is futile in comparison" (TLB). No matter how long we live, it will be like only a few seconds in the grand scope of eternity.

What you do with Jesus Christ determines where you spend eternity. What you do with your time, talents, and treasures determines what rewards you get in eternity. Do you remember the board game called The Game of Life? You got to choose your career and lifestyle, and then at the end of the game, there was Reckoning Day when your choices were evaluated. It's not so far from the way we'll be held accountable for our decisions. What you do with your dash of time here on this earth prepares you for eternity. Until you understand the fact that life is preparation for eternity, life won't make sense to you.

Jess Moody was a young pastor in Owensborough, Kentucky, when he became good friends with a young couple in his church. One day the husband came to Pastor Moody's office clearly distraught and said, "Jess, I've just heard the most awful news. My wife has terminal cancer, and it has spread all over her body. The doctors have just told us she has only weeks, not even months, and, Jess, she's at the hospital, and she's asking for you. We don't know how to handle it. We don't know what to do."

Jess immediately went to the hospital. There the young wife and mother said to him, "I remember in one of your sermons you said a thousand years is like a day to God and a day is unto a thousand years. Is that true? Is a thousand years like a day to God?" The pastor said, "Yes, it's in the Bible." She said, "Good, because I've been doing the math, and I figure if a thousand years is like a day, then forty years is like one hour. I'll be leaving my husband and the children soon. He may live another forty years, but that will be just like an hour to me in heaven. When he gets to heaven, I'll greet him and say, 'Where have you been for an hour? Did you just go to the office, or were you running errands? I've missed you.' My children may live another seventy or eighty years, but that will be like two hours to me. When they get to heaven, I'll greet them and say, 'How was school today? Mom misses you when you're gone for a couple of hours. I wonder how you are doing, because mommies don't like to be away from their children long.'"

Jess Moody said two weeks later she went to be with the Lord, and the last thing she said to her husband was "I love you. Take care of my children. I'll see you in an hour." Now that's an eternal perspective. That's the real perspective that can motivate each of us to live the one-month-to-live lifestyle for years to come.

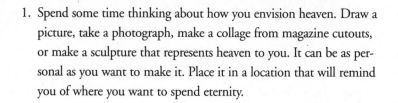

Make It Last for Life

1. Spend some time thinking about how you envision heaven. Draw a picture, take a photograph, make a collage from magazine cutouts, or make a sculpture that represents heaven to you. It can be as personal as you want to make it. Place it in a location that will remind you of where you want to spend eternity.

2. In your journal or other safe place, write a scene in which you imagine meeting God in heaven for the first time. What would you want to say to Him? ask Him? hear Him say to you? Spend some time in prayer, sharing your thoughts with the One who loves you most.

3. What eternal investment have you made this week? How much time have you spent engaged with God's Word? How much time connecting with people in ways that matter most? Set an eternal goal for yourself—something you want to do that will stand the test of time, someone you want to invest in—and find the time to pursue it in the coming week.

Game On

LIVING IT UP

> Here is the test to find
> whether your mission on Earth is finished:
> If you're alive, it isn't.
> —RICHARD BACH

> Though no one can go back and make a brand-new start,
> anyone can start now and make a brand-new ending.
> —CARL BARD

*S*ince you're reading this last chapter in our exploration of living the one-month-to-live lifestyle, you know your time is *not* up. God willing, you will live for many, many more months, years, or decades, enjoying life to the fullest, forever changed as you embrace who He has made you to be and your passionate pursuit of its fulfillment.

This, in a nutshell, is the entire premise of the book. You have been given an extraordinary gift—your life. You have an exceptional calling—to be the very best *you* God created you to be. Your goal is to unwrap this gift and use all that you've been given in the pursuit of what matters most—loving God and loving other people.

Passion Play

As we conclude our journey together in these pages, I want to offer you one last word. If I were limited to only one thing that you would take from this book, it would be to ignite and restore passion to your life. If you only had one month to live, you would want to enjoy every single moment as the precious gift it is. And you would want to make every second count toward something meaningful and eternal, something that fulfills your purpose on this earth. The fuel for sustaining the one-month-to-live lifestyle over the long haul is passion.

Nothing great ever happens without passion. The driving force behind all masterful art, all moving music, all classic literature, all powerful drama, all stunning architecture is passion. Passion propels athletes to break records. Passion pushes scientists to discover new cures for diseases. Passion drives us to share the love of God in creative, innovative ways with those around us. Passion is what gives life to life.

God intends for us to live passionately. "So love the Lord God with all your passion and prayer and intelligence and energy" (Mark 12:30, MSG). We were made with the capacity for passion because God is a passionate God, and we're made in His image. We're told, "Never be lacking in zeal, but keep your spiritual fervor, serving the Lord" (Romans 12:11). Notice the word "keep"; it tells us that passion is something we can lose. If we don't work at it, the stresses and pressures of life can steal our passion for our families, friends, and careers.

One Life to Live

In order to keep our passion alive and thriving, we must be sure to include its four key ingredients. The first piece of the passion puzzle is the most important—love. Love is the foundation of a passionate, purposeful life. The fuel that fires the passion in a marriage relationship is love. The fuel that fires productivity at the workplace is love. The fuel that keeps us growing in our relationship with God is love. Not obligation or legalistic obedience. Love.

What if you don't feel as passionate about God as you once did, you don't have the spiritual fervor you once had? Then you have to start doing the things you did when you first fell in love with God. What did you do? You spent time with Him. You were so excited about the Bible and about learning what it means to love God. You told everybody what was going on in your life. You told your friends what

God was doing in your life. You have to get back to doing those things if you want to fall in love with God all over again. If you want to rekindle your passion for life, then focus on God's love for you.

The next essential in a passionate life is integrity. While people may define this term in a variety of ways, integrity is simply uniting what we say we believe with the way we live. Just as lust destroys the passion in our lives, so does a lack of integrity. Nothing dilutes our passion more than when we say we believe something but don't live it out. When we say our health is important but we consistently overeat unhealthy foods, we lose integrity. When we say our families are important but we're always working and are never present, we lose heart. When we say we love God as the foundation for our lives but we don't relate to Him on a daily basis, we suffer. Our hearts become divided, and we lose the primary focus of our lives. If you want to live passionately, then you must live a congruent life, acting according to what you believe is true.

The next element essential to sustaining passion is forgiveness. In each of the four sections of this book, forgiveness has emerged in one form or another as a vital part of the one-month-to-live lifestyle. Nothing drains passion quicker than unresolved conflict. Job 5:2 tells us, "Surely resentment destroys the fool, and jealousy kills the simple" (NLT). These two—resentment and jealousy—will steal passion quicker than anything else.

Resentment is the great passion killer. This is why God says we must learn to forgive others. If you want to restore your passion for life, you have to learn to forgive people. When we carry around resentment, bitterness, and hurt, they corrode our lives. The people who hurt us don't suffer any consequences. We're not getting back at them at all. Those negative emotions just hurt us and drain us of our passion for life. Jesus is the great example for us here, as He always is. On the cross, what did He say? "Father, forgive them, for they do not know what they are doing" (Luke 23:34). He forgave those who were crucifying Him. No one forgave more than Jesus Christ. He was the most passionate person who ever lived, because He was the most forgiving person who ever lived.

Finally, we need enthusiasm to maintain our passion in life. The word *enthusiasm* comes from two Greek words: *en* and *theos*. *Theos* is the Greek word for "God," and *en* simply means "in," so literally it means "God within." If you want to live each and every day as if it were your last, then you must focus on your relationship with God. If you struggle with passion in your life, perhaps you aren't cultivating your relationship with Him at the level for which you were designed. We have a spiritual hunger within us, one that is never satisfied until we rest in God. We can chase all kinds of things to fulfill us and make us happy, but only One satisfies us. If we want to live the rest of our lives as if we only had one month left, then we would want to know that God is in us, in the details of every day. We would want to experience the intimacy of His love for us and to share it with those around us.

Love. Integrity. Forgiveness. Enthusiasm. *Life*. The passionate life, the one life we've been given to live. It's about living with this passion, living life to the fullest and not settling. It's about living passionately, loving completely, learning humbly, and leaving a legacy that will have eternal impact. If you only had one month to live, isn't this how you'd want to live—knowing you squeezed every second of life for all it was worth, enjoying the abundant (not the safe, easy, or comfortable) life that God promised us?

Our Example

When I look at Jesus' life, I see someone who knew how to live. In fact, Jesus knew how much time He had left. So how did He live when He knew He had one month left on earth? He lived out these four principles that we've looked at. First, He lived passionately. In fact, we call the end of His life the passion of Christ. He lived His life all out, totally for His Father and to make a difference in the world. Jesus was the most passionate person who ever lived, and He wants us to live with that same passion. In John 10:10 He says, "I have come in order that you might have life—life in all its fullness" (GNT).

He wants us to live a life that's filled with the things He has for us. I recently attended the funeral of a dear woman in our church who was in her nineties when she went to be with the Lord, and everyone agreed that she had lived a good, full life. There's a big difference between a full life and a good, full life. Maybe you're living a full life—full of activities and stress and anxiety. But what I'm talking about is a good, full life. This woman lived a life full of compassion, and that's a good, full life.

Jesus also loved completely. John 13:1 says, "Jesus knew that the time had come for him to leave this world and go to the Father. Having loved his own who were in the world, he now showed them the full extent of his love." So what did

Jesus do when He knew He only had one month to live? He loved completely the people He was closest to. He focused on the relationships that mattered most—His disciples. And in the same way, we can love completely by focusing with high intensity on those relationships that are most important in our lives. It never ceases to amaze me how much intentionality I need to pour into my relationships with my family in order to really connect. It takes being intentional every single day with each one of our children and with each other in our marriage and in every other relationship that is important to us for those relationships to thrive.

The third principle in the one-month-to-live lifestyle is to learn humbly, and Jesus was our greatest example of humility. Philippians 2:8 says, "He humbled himself and became obedient to death—even death on a cross!" Jesus was God Himself, and yet He humbled Himself, wrapped Himself in human flesh, and became one of us so we could experience God.

The fourth universal principle is to leave boldly, and again Jesus is our greatest example as He left an eternal legacy here on this earth, and He left boldly and went to be with His Father. He was ready to go. Luke 9:51 says, "As the time drew near for his return to heaven, Jesus resolutely set out for Jerusalem" (NLT). Jesus went to the cross boldly. He was resolute in going to the cross because of His love for us. We can leave a bold legacy on earth as well and spend our days on something that will far outlast us.

When my mom was about the age I am now, she found out that she had cancer, and it wasn't long until she was told she had one month to live. But the beautiful thing was that she had nothing to change. From the day she heard those words, she kept on living the same way. Why? Because she had been living intentionally all along. She'd been loving the people in her life completely. She'd been doing the things she needed to do. She hadn't left things unsaid that she needed to say. So when she found out she had one month left, she was able to continue down the same path. My goal for you and for me is that we will live intentionally so we will have no regrets. I pray that when you and I reach our last day on this earth, we will know that we have lived completely the life we were made for.

One of the mysteries of life is that none of us knows when we're going to die. But it's a fact that we will die. "Man's days are determined; you have decreed the number of his months" (Job 14:5). If we're willing to accept this and trust God with the end point of our time on this earth, then we can focus on how we fill in that dash between the year we were born and the year we will die. We can make our dash an incredible adventure of discovery, joy, and purposeful contentment. We can *live*.

My hope for you is that this book has changed your life, that it has made you think about what it means to live passionately and purposefully like never before. My prayer for you is that God will use all that is true on these pages to inspire you to a new level of living. My challenge to you is to live every day as if you had one month to live!

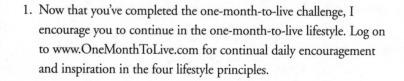

Make It Last for Life

1. Now that you've completed the one-month-to-live challenge, I encourage you to continue in the one-month-to-live lifestyle. Log on to www.OneMonthToLive.com for continual daily encouragement and inspiration in the four lifestyle principles.

2. As soon as possible, plan a day when you can go away by yourself to review and reflect on your experience of reading this book. Make it a one-month-to-live assessment day. Go over the responses, thoughts, and feelings you had as you read this book. What has made the greatest impact on you during this month? Why? How has reading this book and applying it to your life changed you?

3. Get together with at least one friend over coffee or lunch, and share your experience from the past month. Ask what they would do if they knew they only had one month to live.

Inspiring Stories

The following are inspiring stories from people who's lives have been changed by taking the one-month-to-live challenge.

Alan and Karen

A: In June, Karen and I celebrated our twenty-sixth anniversary. It was our dream anniversary vacation. It was something we'd looked forward to for all of our marriage. We were so excited because we got to go to Maui.

I think the reason our twenty-sixth anniversary was so amazing to me was because I was rediscovering my passion for life. I felt like I had really lost it. I had gotten so preoccupied with making a living, I felt like I was losing my life, or at least my passion for it.

I think the turning point for me was when we were at Karen's parents' fiftieth anniversary celebration; they took a family portrait of us. When we received the photo I looked at it and that became a major turning point. I had to get off the dive. I realized I was letting myself go, physically and spiritually. And so I was presented with this challenge by our pastor: What would you do if you had only thirty days left to live? I thought, you know, if I can't honor God with my body, how can I honor him with my heart?

So I took this challenge on to get back in shape, to shed some of the pounds I had gained.

K: Well, the best part of this challenge was obviously losing the weight. Together, we have lost over a hundred pounds—more than fifty pounds each. And that's been incredible. I mean, I feel better, I'm more prone to do things with my kids, and enjoy life a little bit more too.

A: But then, all of a sudden, one Saturday when I was running and working out, I felt something strange in my chest. I came in from my run and I was doing a light workout in the garage. Karen came out and she said, "You okay?" And I said, "Yeah, I just feel a little funny in my chest."

I ate a meal and then I went to church that Saturday night. In between the two services on Saturday night I went in to see Pastor Kerry and said, "I think I'm going to have to go home. I'm not going to be able to serve in the next service. I'm not feeling well." He asked me what was wrong. I said, "I feel kind of cold and clammy. I've had a little bit of pain down my left arm." He immediately said, "You go to the emergency room." W hen I got there, they ran the typical tests and said, "Aw, things don't look too bad. We'll just wait for the doctor." I waited about three hours, while my wife finished serving at church. Then she called me, "Hey, where are you?" I said, "Well, I'm at the hospital." She asked, "Who are you visiting?" I replied, "Well, I'm in the emergency room." I then told her what happened. She came and sat with me until the doctor could see me. After they ran more tests, the doctor said, "You've had an event sometime today and we need to take this serious and check it out. You had a heart attack."

I said, "Doc, it's not that I'm a little bit bitter, but I've just lost about fifty pounds. I'm working out, I eat healthy, I don't drink, I don't smoke, you know, I work at a church. What's up with getting a heart attack? I feel like I need to go back and eat burgers and fries again." He laughed and said, "Look at it like this: Had you not lost that weight, this heart attack could have been fatal or given you permanent heart damage."

The moment the doctor said I had a heart attack and that there was no doubt about it, it was amazing, the peace I felt inside. But when I saw Karen sitting in the chair beside me, I kept thinking of all the weight that would fall on her shoulders and that responsibility. I know she carries a lot, but to carry that alone was unimaginable to me and unfair to her. I was so thankful that God gave me a second chance, and that this thing worked out, and that we could move on with our lives together. I'm just so thankful for Karen and for her support. I love her..

K: I'm definitely glad that I took the challenge. It has changed our lives, our marriage, and our family; it's made us appreciate each other so much more.

A: I'm so thankful that just from a simple challenge we took some steps of action together, and it drew us closer together. It revived the passion in my life for what I do and for who I am as a husband and as a father. I'm enjoying the moments more than I ever enjoyed them before. So if you're considering the challenge, take it. What would you do if you had thirty days left to live? Because it could save your life.

"One thing I changed was learning to text message in order to maintain a more regular contact with my grandchildren. Six out of eight of them text, and the other two can't wait until they have their own cell phones."
—Jim

Ragan McDaniel

When Pastor Kerry gave the one-month-to-live challenge, I decided to take a moment and think of the things that I do now, and the things that I would like to do different. I decided I wanted to surprise my son at school for lunch. So I stopped and picked up a couple of Happy Meals. He had no idea I was coming. I thought it would be a fun thing to do for my eight-year-old son and that he'd get a kick out of it. I checked in at the front office and went into the lunchroom. As I rounded the corner, he had his back to me, but his friends were kind of looking and pointing. Well, he turned around and his face just lit up. It's a vision that I'll never forget. Just the sight of his face is implanted on my heart and my brain forever. When he lined up with his class to go back to his room, I decided, you know, I'm gonna walk back to the room with him, just to say good-bye and every-thing. Usually when I drop him off or walk him in to class, he says, "Oh, there's Dad. See you later, Dad." But this was different. We started walking down the hallway, and he reached over and grabbed my hand—it's a feeling that you can't really.... It's hard to put into words without getting emotional. To have him just reach and grab my hand and walk with me all the way to his class was an experi-ence that I'll cherish for the rest of my life.

The one-month-to-live challenge has also strengthened my relationship with my wife. Coming home from work, or whereever it would be, we would always greet each other with a kiss and a hello, and how was your day—something sim-ple, more of a small talk. But now we take the time to listen to each other, and to focus on what the other person needs and what is important to them. Sometimes we do something as simple as just walking around the block, just her and I.

My mother and father were divorced when I was really young, and I blamed my father for not being a dad and not having a relationship. I see him every day at work, but we just don't have a good father-son relationship. But, you know, after Pastor Kerry's challenge, I decided…I'm waiting on him to be a dad, but I'm also not being a son. It's given me no regrets because I don't have to sit and blame him; I don't have to point fingers anymore. I've taken the steps to be a son, which has helped him be a better father. Our relationship between us has grown. We go to lunch together now. We laugh, we talk, we talk on the telephone outside of work. And we never did that in the past for so many years. I realized how much I missed that.

The one-month-to-live challenge helped me take initiative instead of waiting. You don't know how much time you have, so why sit and wait? I wanted to focus on how I treat others, and do it immediately because what I'm leaving behind is my legacy. And if I don't work on that, then who's going to work on it?

"I am going to start doing a Bible study with teen girls on this book. It's never too late to start living in the now… I can't say enough about how much this book changed my viewpoint. I am enjoying every day with my children and getting my priorities in order." —Amazon.com reviewer

Jimmy and Betty

B: When I first found out about *One Month to Live*, it just so happened that we were in the hospital with my husband and we had just received notice that his cancer had returned.

When he was told that he only had the six to ten weeks to live, or if his chemo worked, eighteen to twenty-four months, he was so calm.

J: I had the most amazing calm peace that came over me.

B: I didn't understand that at the time.

J: God gave me the peace to accept what I was told. I don't know if it'll be six weeks. I don't know if it'll be twenty-four months—or what it will be. I don't really think about it because that peace and that feeling that I had at that time was so astounding. *One Month to Live* is so personal to me because of that. And I tell you what, I'm really grateful.

B: I think the thirty-day challenge gives you a great way to get closer to God. It has for me. I have talked to God a lot lately. And I think that anybody who can really get into these shoes and do this will have a better relationship with God.

J: For a person who is considering the one-month-to-live challenge, I would say you'll think about your life a lot. All the things that you've done, the opportunities that you took, the opportunities that you missed—that you let go. Because when you get to the situation like I'm in it's very easy to love God because you don't have any distractions. And during your life, you have your life to live, so there are a lot of things that distract you. You don't think about God nearly as much as what I do. I don't have a lot of regrets or anything like that, but the thing about it is, now I feel so thankful that God has allowed me to have the things I have and to do the things that I have done. For someone considering doing the *One Month to Live* like that, I would say think about the things God has done for you. They're good things.

"I have found the ability to forgive those that I could not before, my job seems to have a higher purpose for me (and I look forward to going to work now), and I feel as though I am living more stress-free now."
—D. Pfeffer, Texas

Denise Greene

I don't want to have a *regrets life*. When I get to be eighty or ninety, I want to look back and say I really lived. When I heard about *One Month to Live,* I thought, "What things do I need to change in my life to really live like I want to live?" The first thing I thought of was the one thing I didn't want to do the most, which was forgive my ex-husband for leaving me to be a single mom of a little bitty kid. And that was actually one of the first things I did. That made a big, big difference.

I would encourage anyone doing this to really take it to heart, internalize it, and make it real. Make it a part of your life. For me it was forgiving people I thought had harmed me, letting it go, and finding peace with all these situations in my life that I didn't like. And it was also about finding joy and happiness in the little things, like eating dinner with my little girl at our Dora the Explorer table. I mean, how much simpler can it be? And how much more wonderful can that be? Coloring with her, playing with our little Play-Doh—little things I've learned to take to heart.

I sat down and I really looked at all the different things I would want to do if I seriously knew I had thirty days to live. What would I change? It was a lot of forgiveness. It was a lot of finding joy and peace and happiness in the little things— the everyday little things. I've really learned to enjoy every single moment I have with my little girl. Even if I have thirty more years to go, she's only going to be two once. I only have this little moment with her. So, even though I'm a single mom, on a commission income—so the more I work, the more money I make— it doesn't matter. I've turned that over to God. I leave as late as possible, and I pick her up as early as possible, and I spend as much time with her, because she's what's really important. If I only had thirty days left to live, I would literally just quit my job and wish them all well in a nice, sweet way and be done with it. I would spend it all with my kid. Why should I spend all of the time I have while she's two working? It just doesn't make any sense to me.

Also, I started journaling for my daughter. If I only had thrity days to go, I would want to leave a legacy for her. She won't have a mom if I'm not here, so I want her to have a God that she can lean on. I'm journaling to her the things that happen to me in everyday life and how God helps me through those situations or how God is there for me to help me rejoice in the things that are wonderful.

A girlfriend of mine just had her nineteen-year-old daughter die—out of the blue. She was in a car accident on a regular, old Saturday night. You never ever know how much time you have, so I think this is a good opportunity to take the time we have and really live it.